The Hungry Woman

THE HUNGRY WOMAN

Myths and Legends of the

AZTECS

Edited by John Bierhorst

With illustrations by

Aztec artists of the Sixteenth Century

William Morrow and Company

New York 1984

Designed by Jane Byers Bierhorst
Printed in the United States of America.

10 9 8 7 6 5 4 3 2 1

Library of Congress Cataloging in Publication Data

Bierhorst, John | The hungry woman.

Bibliography: p.
Summary: Narratives from Aztec Indian lore.
1. Aztecs—Legends.   2. Indians of Mexico—Legends.
3. Aztecs—Religion and mythology—Juvenile literature.
[1. Aztecs—Legends.   2. Indians of Mexico—Legends]
I. Title.
F1219.76.F65B54   1984   398.2'0972   83-25068
ISBN 0-688-02766-0

CONTENTS

After Cortés

The Hungry Woman

Introduction

Recorded in the sixteenth century shortly after the Spanish Conquest, the Aztec narratives that can be read today are of the kind that had once been recited by court historians and illustrated by official painters in bark-paper books. Their themes are the creation of the world and the rise and fall of cities. Campfire yarns, animal stories, and tales of anonymous heroes, common in modern folktale collections and undoubtedly familiar to the Aztecs, are here lacking—for the simple reason that no one thought to write them down. The science of folklore, with its emphasis on the unschooled and the unofficial, would not be born for another three hundred years.

Those who took charge of collecting the old traditions were the missionary friars, assisted by students recruited from what was left of the Aztec nobility. Skilled in the new art of writing Nahuatl, or Aztec, in European script, they interviewed reputable elders and found out what the native people had known of their past and what gods had been worshipped. The most diligent of the friars, the Franciscan Bernardino de Sahagún, explained that he "sifted" his writings three times. In other words, once he had taken down a particular text, he checked it with a second and even a third informant to be sure it was authoritative, making any necessary changes along the way. Armed with a full understanding of the old religion, the friars could then refute it more easily. This at least was their justification in an age when all learning was supposed to serve the Church. It is generally recognized, however, that their remarkable studies of Aztec religion, history, and language were part of the much broader quest that had been responsible for Columbus' voyages and was already changing the intellectual climate of Europe. In the spirit of modern inquiry, the friars were expanding their knowledge of the world.

Although the missionaries worked in Texcoco, Tlalmanalco, Xochimilco, and other formerly Aztec cities, their greatest activity was in the city of Mexico, home of the Mexica, whose king had been the "great king" over all the rest. As a result, the myths and legends that were recorded deal largely with matters of interest to these Mexica, or Mexicans. They, like all Aztecs, understood the story of the world as a repeating pattern, to be studied partly as a means of savoring past glories and partly to find out what might lie ahead.

Cycles of history

According to several of the native accounts, the sun was created and destroyed four times before the beginning of the present age. Of particular interest to the mythmakers was the time of darkness between the fourth and fifth suns. This was when human life received its final form and the gods established the custom of human sacrifice. With the creation of the fifth sun, the mythic period draws to a close and we enter a legendary time that gradually becomes historical in the modern sense.

Aztec legends, as opposed to myths, begin with the civilization of the Toltecs, whose capital, Tula, flourished for three or four hundred years until the late twelfth century. Although archaeologists have established that Tula took its culture from the metropolis known as Teotihuacan (about 150 B.C.–A.D. 850), Aztec legends portray the Toltecs as the inventors of all arts and sciences and their capital as a place of unprecedented splendor. Every Aztec city wished to be another Tula. However, the actual details of Tula's history were obscured by contradictory records, and for the most part the legends tell of its decline, concentrating on the omens and fantastic calamities that signaled the end.

After the fall of Tula, tribes from the north moved into the region the Toltecs had dominated, intermarried with the town dwellers already established there, and adopted the Toltec language, called Nahuatl ("that which is strong and clear"). The new culture that developed has been called Aztec by historians and anthropologists. But the people themselves preferred to

5

identify with particular city-states, calling each other Huexotzincans, Mexicans, Xochimilcans, and so forth.

In the case of the Mexicans, the founding of their city came late. By the time they arrived in what would eventually be known as the Valley of Mexico, nearly all the territory had been staked out. Unable to find a choice upland site, they were forced to settle on marshy islands in the middle of one of the large lakes that covered the floor of the valley. Although this was a difficult period for the Mexica, in later years the troubles they suffered in founding their capital were glorified in what is perhaps the most important series of strictly Mexican legends.

As the city grew, its armies gained a reputation for fierceness, enabling Mexico to assume an increasing role in the politics of the region. By 1440 the great triple alliance of Mexico, Texcoco, and Tlacopan had been formed, preparing the way for conquests throughout the valley and beyond. Within the alliance, the superior strength of the Mexicans gave them a commanding position, so that by the end of the century their king was in effect the emperor over the entire Aztec realm, which now stretched from the Pacific Ocean to the Gulf Coast and south to Guatemala.

It was under the fourth ruler, Itzcoatl, that the empire began to take shape, reaching its greatest extent under the ninth king, Montezuma II, also called Montezuma the Younger, or simply Montezuma. Although he was not the last of Mexico's kings, Montezuma was the last to rule as emperor. At the time of his death, in June of 1520, the subject states were already defecting to the Spaniards, who had arrived a year earlier. Cuitlahuac, who reigned for three months after the death of Montezuma, died of smallpox brought by the conquerors, and his successor, Cuauhtemoc, ruled the city of Mexico as a fortress under siege, surrendering to the Spaniards in August of 1521. Despite the drama of these events, the only genuinely legendary narratives that recall the Conquest period are those that tell of the talking stone, the wound, the dreams, and the various other omens that plagued Montezuma in the last years of his reign.

From the preceding summary it is apparent that the bursts of creative fiction are clustered at the turning points in Aztec chronology: the creation of the fifth sun, the fall of Tula, the founding of Mexico, and the last days of Montezuma. The tellers of myths and legends were interested in the end of an old cycle or the beginning of a new one. At such times the fate of the world hung in the balance. And those were the times when the gods intervened.

Quetzalcoatl and Tezcatlipoca

The two most important spirits in Aztec stories are Quetzalcoatl and Tezcatlipoca. Cooperating on rare occasions, they usually oppose one another, with Quetzalcoatl taking the role of the creator and Tezcatlipoca the destroyer. They work together to form the earth, then compete for the honor of being the sun. After the flood that ends the fourth age, they come together again to lift the sky to its former position.

During the great days of Tula, the two gods descend to earth, one as benefactor, the other as troublemaker. Under the leadership of Quetzalcoatl, the Toltecs discover all the useful arts, find jewels, and grow giant vegetables. Wise and righteous, their leader lives the life of a priest. In the midst of this perfection, Tezcatlipoca appears as a sorcerer who robs the people of their senses, organizing dangerous nighttime dances at the edge of a cliff and spreading an odor of death. Quetzalcoatl himself is persuaded to burn the city and run away.

In the next round of stories the leader who helps the newly arrived Aztecs, it might be supposed, will be Tezcatlipoca; and in fact a few fragmentary tales from the cities of Amaquemecan and Texcoco show this to be the case. The only legends of Aztec beginnings that are at all well preserved, however, are the ones from Mexico, and in these the role of Tezcatlipoca is played by the Mexican tribal god, Huitzilopochtli. Like Tezcatlipoca, Huitzilopochtli is harsh and warlike. But he is a much simpler god, concerned not with the larger questions of human fate but with the conquests that will make his people masters of the world. Speaking to them in dreams, he guides them to the mystical eagle perched on the prickly pear—to be made famous centuries later as the symbol of modern Mexico—and instructs them to found the city that will become their stronghold.

Quetzalcoatl appears to have been forgotten. But when the Mexicans are at the height of their power, familiar-sounding rumors from the east begin to reach the capital. Men with beards have come over the ocean

(Quetzalcoatl was bearded, and he took his departure over the same ocean). The strangers (not unlike the Toltecs) have a rich technology. Moreover, it is the year 1519 (1 Reed, according to the Aztec calendar, a year traditionally associated with Quetzalcoatl). Convinced that the event has been predetermined, Montezuma greets the Spanish leader, Hernando Cortés, as though he were the returning god and surrenders the throne of Mexico without a struggle.

Some of the traditional narratives connected with this final episode, like the tale of the talking stone, are as fabulous as one could wish. Others are real enough. The rumors of bearded strangers turned out to be true, and Montezuma actually did believe that Cortés was either Quetzalcoatl or his representative.

The dangerous woman

Though kings, priests, and male deities predominate, Aztec lore is noteworthy for its robust female figures, who are as adventurous as the males and have the power to threaten them. One of the best known is Coyolxauhqui (She Wears War Bells as Her Female Cosmetic). In the story of Huitzilopochtli's birth, she leads a war party against the god's mother in an attempt to prevent him from being born. Another strong female is the witch Malinalxochitl (Twist Flower), who kills men at a glance. Like Coyolxauhqui, she is said to be a sister of Huitzilopochtli. In both cases the woman is portrayed as the tyrannical leader of the Mexicans, whom Huitzilopochtli must get rid of in order to assert his own authority and set Mexico on the path of empire.

Still more fearsome, if less active, is the so-called woman of discord, the goddess who cooperates with Huitzilopochtli by demanding conquests. Also called Our Grandmother (Toci), this deity belongs to a group of closely related earth spirits that were no doubt worshipped throughout the Aztec realm under one name or another, often simply as Our Mother (Tonantzin). In Mexican lore the goddess typically craves human blood, especially the blood of sacrificed enemy prisoners. Sometimes she is said to have mouths all over her body, and sometimes she can be heard at night, crying to be fed.

On the northern outskirts of Mexico, at a little hill called Tepeyacac, there was a shrine of Tonantzin that attracted pilgrims from as far away as fifty miles. Whether they came out of fear or to ask blessings would be hard to say. It seems unlikely, however, that ordinary people would have made such a trip to pray for war, though priests and kings might have done so. In any case, we do know that the earth goddess had another face. As Snake Woman, who helped Quetzalcoatl create human life, she could be benevolent; as Snake Skirt (Cihuacoatl), she was the virgin mother of Huitzilopochtli; and even as the hungry woman with many mouths, she provided grass, forests, pools, springs, and flowers.

Within a few years after the Conquest, a cult of the Virgin Mary that had originally been established at Guadalupe, Spain, found its way to the New World, and a shrine in her honor was set up at Tepeyacac, perhaps with the intention of replacing the cult of Tonantzin. Indian worshippers, nevertheless, kept the name Tonantzin when praying to the new virgin.

By the middle of the seventeenth century the Guadalupe cult had become important enough to have a legend of its own, which was provided by Luis Lasso de la Vega, curate of the church at Tepeyacac. Although Lasso de la Vega wrote the story in Nahuatl, borrowing phrases from the Aztec literature that had been preserved by Sahagún and others during the preceding century, there is no evidence that he copied it from early sources or that it had been composed by an Aztec. It is included in the present collection because of its significance for modern Mexico and because it is widely believed to be an Aztec account of real events.

Without the legend, which tells how the Virgin appeared to a poor Indian named Juan Diego, the cult would probably not have grown as it did. A symbol of national unity, drawing worshippers from all ethnic groups and all walks of life, Guadalupe today is the most popular shrine in Mexico. Just as in the sixteenth century, it attracts Nahuatl-speaking pilgrims who address the Virgin as Tonantzin. Famous for her cures, Tonantzin has become a lady of mercy.

But the old, grim aspect of the earth goddess survives too. Known as *la llorona* (the weeping woman), she still haunts the countryside, crying in the night. Sometimes she is identified with Malintzin, the Indian woman who served Cortés as both interpreter and mistress. Usually she is said to have murdered her children, and her cry is ¡*Ay, mis hijos!* (Alas, my children!)—although on the eve of the Spanish Conquest she is supposed to have cried out to her living children as an omen of disaster ("My children, already we're passing away," or "My children, where can I take you?"). In many of the stories her weeping seduces men, luring them to the edge of a cliff or some other dangerous place.

In a country where nearly everyone claims part-Indian descent, the legendary *llorona,* still alive in popular tradition, is of more than passing interest, especially when it is remembered that the original Indian ancestor was in most cases a woman, taken with the spoils of the Conquest. Significantly, the great male deities of Aztec lore have been dead for centuries. Few if any storytellers know the deeds of Quetzalcoatl, Tezcatlipoca, and Huitzilopochtli. It is the figure of a woman, therefore, whether as Tonantzin or as *la llorona,* who takes modern Mexico back to its native roots.

Oral literature

The verbal art of the imperial Aztecs was necessarily an oral, not a written, literature. Until the arrival of the Spaniards, who taught the use of alphabetic writing, storytellers had had to rely on memory and word of mouth, helped by picture books that may be compared to modern comics without words. In addition to narrative, or *tlanonotzaliztli,* the important categories were *huehuetlatolli* (word of the elders) and *cuicatl* (song).

The term *huehuetlatolli,* used as the title of a collection of formal Aztec speeches published in 1600, has lately been applied to all the elegant oratory with which the Aztecs greeted visitors, addressed gods, or admonished their children. Set phrases, and perhaps entire speeches, were memorized word for word and passed along from one generation to the next. Such an expression as "I have been expecting you for as many days as there are fingers on my two hands" (literally, "I have been expecting you for five, for ten")—see page 56 of this book, also page 110—provides an example of the typically ornate style. Montezuma's long speech on page 110 has been called a *huehuetlatolli.* But often such speeches are even longer, requiring ten or twenty minutes to recite.

As for the *cuicatl,* or songs, most of the texts that have been preserved are of the kind that were accompanied by the *huehuetl* (a sort of tom-tom) and the *teponaztli* (a two-toned drum carved from a short, hollowed-out log). These instruments are shown in the illustration on page 118. Usually dancing was included, sometimes with masks, pantomime, and stage props, creating a kind of theater. War is the general theme, typically covered up in fanciful figures of speech involving birds and flowers. Translated, the words strike the modern eye as poetry. Some of the songs pay honor to the gods; most celebrate the deeds of ancestors, recalling important battles.

In the 1550s and 1560s, traditional singers revitalized the *cuicatl,* introducing Christian themes, the theme of the Conquest itself, and a more elaborate imagery. The song summoning the ghost of Montezuma, on page 117, may be taken as an example of the new style. The art of narrative also enjoyed a mid-century revival, producing elaborate accounts of the Conquest and the tales of

Montezuma's last days. After this period of late flowering, the verbal arts declined rapidly.

As in earlier times, the mid-century narrators focused on the great themes of war and empire. What tales were traded by villagers or heard at bedtime from the lips of grandmothers we will never know. Aztec culture, nurtured in the urban households of kings, nobles, and rich merchants, died without recording the voices of ordinary people.

In the nineteenth century, when folklorists began collecting narratives in Nahuatl-speaking villages of the central highlands, they found little that could be connected to the imperial lore preserved in the decades following the Conquest. Modern Nahuatl folktales tend to be animal stories, adaptations of European fairy tales, and legends about local heroes. Nevertheless, there are unmistakable echoes of the past, as in the frequent mention of a paradise called Tlalocan (the home of the Aztec rain god) or in the reappearance of such names as Montezuma and Malintzin, sometimes applied to local heroes and heroines.

The myths and legends

In a language as rich in synonyms as Nahuatl, the word *tlanonotzaliztli* (that which informs) cannot have been the only term for narrative. In fact, the sixteenth-century dictionary of Alonso Molina also lists *tenonotzaliztli* (that which informs people), *tlatolli* (word), and *tlatolpohualiztli* (word recounting). But it will be noticed that these terms are vague; at least some apply equally well to oratory or even song. *Tlaquetzalli* (story) is more specific, but extends the category to tales told for entertainment; and *zazanilli* (trifle) applies only to jokes, animal stories, and what Molina calls old wives' tales. Unfortunately, there are no recorded Aztec *zazanilli*—though the term was applied to a collection of Aesop's *Fables* translated into Nahuatl in the late 1500s.

Lacking a clearer insight into native usage, we could simply do as folklorists do and divide the material into "legends" (stories believed to be true by the people who tell them) and "folktales" (stories not believed to be true). By this standard, no Aztec folktales have survived, and every narrative in this book would have to be called a legend.

But if we take an objective view, Aztec lore fits just as well into traditional literary terminology, allowing us to speak of myth, legend, and history, where myth deals with fabulous events in a timeless past, legend combines the historical with the fabulous, and history sticks closely to the facts. Possibly the Aztecs themselves separated myths from narratives that were genuinely historical. If so, there was an opposite tendency to invent dates for mythic events, just as Europeans once imagined that Adam and Eve had been expelled from Eden exactly five thousand years before the birth of Christ. Moreover, as already pointed out, myth established a pattern for cycles of history that continued into the present. Nevertheless, a distinction between recent and ancient events could roughly correspond to our categories of "myth" and "history." It is all but certain, however, that the Aztecs did not divide history from legend as here defined.

At least two of the narratives in this book, "The Return of Quetzalcoatl" and "Is It You?" both documenting Cortés' arrival, qualify as history in the modern sense—history told by a people whose fantasies had become real. Cortés' spectacular entry into sixteenth-century Mexico would be comparable, today, to a landing by creatures from outer space. Another story, "The Woman of Discord," *could* be true, bizarre as it seems. Thus the distinction between history and legend may be hard to draw, even if one tries to be objective.

Among the many sixteenth-century sources of Aztec myths, legends, and histories, the best known is Sahagún's *General History of the Things of New Spain*, preserved in fragments at libraries in Madrid and in a complete copy, called the *Florentine Codex*, at the Laurentian Library in Florence, Italy. Written in Nahuatl and Spanish, in facing columns, the codex includes oratory, songs, descriptions of ceremonies, a history of the Conquest, and the most famous of the Quetzalcoatl legends. Another important source is the so-called *Crónica X*, a lost Nahuatl manuscript known through Spanish versions made by Diego Durán about 1580 and by Hernando Alvarado Tezozomoc about 1600. By far the fullest account of the history of Tenochtitlan, *Crónica X* spins yarn after yarn, re-creating all the great deeds of the Mexican kings, their speeches, and even their conversations. Lesser sources include several, like *Crónica X*, that are known only in Spanish, and one, the "Histoyre du Mechique," that survives in a sixteenth-century French translation.

As suggested earlier, these narratives were not intended as mere entertainment. Although the modern reader may approach them as literature, to the Aztecs they were among the most precious of texts, comparable to the Hebrew Bible or the Christian Gospels. To

read them is to find out what the Aztecs believed about
their world and its destiny.

Often the native storytellers would string narratives
into a loosely connected epic, not unlike the Bible, beginning with the creation of the earth or the first sun
and continuing into historical times. Arranged in the
traditional sequence, the stories in this book are therefore best read in order rather than by skipping back and
forth.

The English versions given here have been made directly from the Nahuatl texts or from the earliest
known Spanish (or French) adaptations, if the originals
have been lost. Stories from *Crónica X* have been re-
constructed using both Durán and Tezozomoc, and in a
few spots a third source, the *Códice Ramírez,* also trace-
able to *Crónica X*. Several other narratives, likewise,
have been adapted from two or more sources, as shown
in the Notes to the Stories.

Those interested in the style of Nahuatl narrative
can get a fairly accurate idea from the selection entitled
"Is It You?," translated word for word from Sahagún.
"Eight Omens," translated faithfully from the same
source, is not as convincingly native. Here it appears
that the narrator, to be obliging, has padded his account with synonyms and explanatory phrases. The fact
is, Sahagún was hoping to write a dictionary and would
often ask his informants to give him different ways of
saying the same thing. No doubt the purest native
texts, stylistically, are those recorded in Nahuatl by Indians working on their own. Such texts are here represented by several selections, including "Up from the
Dead Land" and "Calling the Ghost of Montezuma."

The accompanying pictures, all from the *Florentine*

Codex, were painted by Aztec artists under the direction of Sahagún. With more than a thousand illustrations, ranging from astronomy and zoology to religion and history, the codex serves as a pictorial encyclopedia of Aztec lore. For years the pictures were unavailable except in redrawn versions published by the Mexican scholar Francisco del Paso y Troncoso in the early 1900s. Finally, in 1979, the Mexican government, in cooperation with the Laurentian Library, published a photographic facsimile of the codex (entitled *Códice florentino*), making the pictures available in their original form. Some are in color, some in black and white. The illustrations in this book, uniformly printed in black and white, have been reproduced from the facsimile by permission of the Mexican government.

As will be noticed, these pictures combine the diagramlike quality of Aztec painting with the more realistic European style. Notice also that they are miniatures and that they have the appearance of frames in a comic strip, traits that link them to the Aztec past. Reproduced here as text figures, just as in the *General History* of Sahagún and other manuscripts of the period, they may help modern readers appreciate the unique flavor of sixteenth-century Mexican literature, created by a people determined to preserve their traditions while striving to understand a new way of life.

CREATION
MYTHS

The Hungry Woman

In the place where the spirits live, there was once a woman who cried constantly for food. She had mouths in her wrists, mouths in her elbows, and mouths in her ankles and knees. "She can't eat here," said the other spirits. "She will have to live somewhere else."

But up above, there was only the empty air, and to the right and to the left and in front and behind, it was just the same. In those days the world had not been created. Nevertheless, there was something underneath that seemed to be water. How it had got there nobody knew. "If we put her below," they thought, "then perhaps she will be able to satisfy her hunger."

No sooner had the thought occurred than the spirits Quetzalcoatl and Tezcatlipoca seized the

woman and dragged her down to the water. When they saw that she floated, they changed into snakes, stretching over her in the form of a cross, from right arm to left leg and from left arm to right leg. Catching her hands and feet, they squeezed her from all four directions, pushing so hard that she snapped in half at the waist.

"Now look what we've done," they said, and not knowing what else to do, they carried the bottom half back to the spirit place. "Look," they cried. "What's to be done with this?"

"What a shame," said the other spirits. "But never mind. We'll use it to make the sky." Then, to comfort the poor woman, they all flew down and began to make grass and flowers out of her skin. From her hair they made forests, from her eyes, pools and springs, from her shoulders, mountains, and from her nose, valleys. At last she will be satisfied, they thought. But just as before, her mouths were everywhere, biting and moaning. And still she hasn't changed.

When it rains, she drinks. When flowers shrivel, when trees fall, or when someone dies, she eats. When people are sacrificed or killed in battle, she drinks their blood. Her mouths are always opening and snapping shut, but they are never filled. Sometimes at night, when the wind blows, you can hear her crying for food.

The First Sun

When the earth had been stretched over the water and shaped into mountains and valleys, the spirits began gathering up light to make the sun. As they worked, Tezcatlipoca kept thinking, "I ought to be the sun." But he was dark as a shadow.

When the work was finished, they all stood back to admire what they had done. "This is my chance," thought Tezcatlipoca, and he snatched the newly made sun and tied it around his middle. As he rose into the sky, casting shadows and patches of light, the other spirits looked up and said, "Well, somebody has to be the sun. Let him do what he can." Then they turned around and began to create the first people.

But the people they made were giants, and as they began to walk on the earth, there were constant cries of "Don't fall! Don't fall!" Whenever the giants met one another, the greeting was always "Don't fall!" because if anyone fell he would never be able to get back up. As they wandered from place to place, afraid to stoop down or bend over, the giants had nothing to eat but acorns that they picked from trees.

Now, when the sun reached the top of the sky, the world became suddenly dark, because the sun that the spirits had made had only enough brightness to last half the day. The spirits, it seems, had made a mistake. The people were too big, and the sun was too small.

After thirteen times fifty-two years, Quetzalcoatl
came chasing after Tezcatlipoca with a big stick
and knocked him out of the sky. He fell into the
ocean, changed shape, came out on land as a jaguar, and ate all the people. This was the end of the
first sun, whose name was Jaguar Sun. As a re-
minder of its fall, the constellation of the jaguar
still dips down to the ocean each night.

Monkeys, Turkeys, and Fish

When the first sun had fallen from the sky, Quetzalcoatl took its place and became the sun called
Wind Sun. There were people under this second
sun, but they had only pine nuts to eat. Year after
year they ate nothing but pine nuts, until at last
Tezcatlipoca rose up as a jaguar, ran across the sky,
and gave the Wind Sun a kick from behind. As it
fell, it gained speed and became a windstorm,
sweeping everything off the earth. Trees and
houses disappeared. All the people were blown
away except for a few who remained hanging in
the air, and these were changed into monkeys.

After the second sun had gone, the spirit of rain
moved into the sky and became the sun called

Rain Sun. There were people under this third sun, but they could find no nourishment other than river corn. True corn had not been discovered. At last Quetzalcoatl sent a shower of fire and hot stones that burned the earth. It was so hot, the sun itself went up in flames. The few people who escaped were changed, and when the fire had cooled they ran out over the blackened earth as turkeys.

Quetzalcoatl invited the rain spirit's wife to become the fourth sun, and she said yes. In the time of this fourth sun, called Water Sun, there were many people. But as yet they had nothing to eat except grass corn. True corn had still not been discovered. Year after year they ate grass corn and sat

and stared at the rain. It rained all the time.

Finally, one year, there was so much rain the lakes and rivers rose over the tops of the mountains, and all the people were changed into fish.

It rained so hard, the sky itself fell down on the earth. At last there was no more rain. Then Quetzalcoatl and Tezcatlipoca crawled under the edge of the sky, one on each side, and changed themselves into trees, the Quetzal Willow and the Tezcatl Tree. As these two grew, one on each side of the world, the sky was pushed up until it reached the place where it had been before.

Leaving the trees in position, the two spirits climbed up over the edge, and each one traveled across the sky. Meeting at the center, they stood together and proclaimed themselves rulers of all that they saw.

The path they traveled is the White Road, and it can still be seen in the night sky.

Up from the Dead Land

The flood that had covered the earth had all drained away. But the spirits were troubled. "Who will be the people?" they asked. "The earth is dry,

29

the skies are dry. But who will be the people?"

While they were thinking, Quetzalcoatl went down to the Dead Land beneath the earth, and when he came to the Dead Land Lord and his wife, who were guarding the bones of the dead, he cried, "Give me your bones!"

No answer.

"These valuable bones that you are guarding. I have come to get them."

"Why do you need them?"

"Because the spirits are worried. They keep asking, 'Who will be the people?'"

"Here, take my trumpet," said the Dead Land Lord. "You may have the bones if you can blow this trumpet and circle four times around my beautiful country." But the trumpet was not hollow.

Then Quetzalcoatl whispered to the worms that lived in the Dead Land, "Worms, come hollow out this trumpet." When they had hollowed it out, bees and hornets flew inside and began to buzz.

As Quetzalcoatl circled the Dead Land with the trumpet buzzing, the Dead Land Lord heard him and said, "The bones are yours. Take them." But he said to the dead who were all around him, "Tell this spirit he cannot have the bones forever. After a while he must bring them back."

30

"Our lord says you must bring them back," they all shouted.

"No," said Quetzalcoatl, "they must live forever."

But his inner thoughts warned him, "Don't tell them that. Tell them the bones will come back." "I will bring them back," he cried. Then he quickly gathered the bones of men and the bones of women, wrapped them up, and ran.

"Don't believe him," cried the Dead Land Lord. "If you let them go, they will never come back. Dig him a grave!"

Then the dead people dug a grave for Quetzalcoatl. And as he tried to escape, a flock of quail flew up at him and scared him, so that he stumbled into the grave and fell unconscious.

When he regained his senses, he saw that the bones had been scattered and that the quail had bit

into them and nibbled them. He sobbed and cried out to his inner thoughts, "How will it be?" His thoughts replied, "How will it be? The bones have been nibbled, and after a while they will rot. There will be death. You cannot change it."

He was filled with sadness. But seeing that he was now free to take the bones, he gathered them up, carried them to the place above the sky, and gave them to the spirit called Snake Woman, who ground them to powder and poured them into a jade bowl. Then Quetzalcoatl spilled blood from his body into the bowl, and all the other spirits did the same.

As the bones came to life, the spirits cried, "Born are the people! They will be our servants. We bled for them, they will bleed for us."

True Corn

"What will the people eat?" asked the spirits. "Let corn be discovered." And no sooner had the command been given than Quetzalcoatl noticed a red ant carrying a kernel of true corn.

"Where did you find it?" he asked. But she would not answer him. Again and again he questioned her, until at last she said, "Follow me."

Then Quetzalcoatl changed into a black ant and followed the red ant to the edge of a mountain.

This was Food Mountain, where corn, beans, peppers, and all the other foods had been hidden since the beginning of the world. "Come this way," she said, and she entered a tunnel that led inside.

With the help of the red ant, the black ant dragged corn kernels back to the spirit place, where the other spirits were waiting. When the corn arrived, the spirits chewed it for us and placed it on our lips. In this way we were made strong.

"Now, what will we do with Food Mountain?" asked Quetzalcoatl.

"We will crack it open, so the people can have all the food," said the other spirits.

As they talked, the one called Nanahuatl split the mountain and revealed what was inside. But the rain was jealous, and he and his children rushed in and stole the food before the other spirits could give it to the people. Corn, beans, peppers, sage, everything was stolen.

The rain spirits still have the food that was in Food Mountain. They give back only a part of it each year—and some years less than others—in exchange for human blood.

The Fifth Sun

The world was still dark, and the spirits began to ask each other, "Who will be the sun?" As they talked, they flew down to the earth and built a fire for the one who would be chosen. But they were afraid. As the fire grew hotter, all that could be heard was "Let someone else do it."

While they were excusing themselves, the one called Nanahuatl just stood aside and listened. He was poor, and his body was covered with sores. When at last they noticed him, they all cried, "Nanahuatl will be the sun."

"Oh no!" he said. "I have sores." But they paid no attention and simply ordered him to do penance so that he would become holy.

For four days, while the fire burned, he pricked himself with spines and needles. At the same time he fasted. When the penance was over, they chalked his body to make it white, pasted feathers on his arms, and said, "Don't be afraid. You will soar through the air and light up the world." Then he closed his eyes and jumped into the fire.

After his body had completely burned, he descended to the Dead Land and traveled underground until he reached the earth's edge on the east.

Meanwhile the spirits were watching to see where the sun would rise. Already it was dawn, but the light seemed to be coming from all directions at once. Some watched the north and some watched the south. Others thought the sun would rise in the west. Still others, including Quetzalcoatl, said, "It will rise in the east," and their words were true.

When the sun appeared, it was bright red. It

wobbled back and forth, bursting with light, shining over all the earth. It was so brilliant that no one could look at it without being blinded. But as

35

soon as it appeared, it stopped rising.

Seeing that it would not go into its course, the spirits sent a falcon as their messenger to find out what the trouble was. When the falcon returned, it reported that the sun would rise no farther until the spirits sacrificed themselves, allowing their hearts to be removed.

Angry and frightened, they called out to the morning star and told him to shoot the sun with one of his arrows. But the sun ducked, and the arrow flew by without hitting its mark.

Then the sun turned to the morning star and shot at him with its flame-colored darts. Wounded, the morning star fell back to the Dead Land. And the spirits, now realizing that the sun's power was too great to resist, took off their clothes and allowed themselves to be sacrificed, one by one. Satisfied at last, Nanahuatl began his journey across the sky.

This was the fifth sun, called Earthquake Sun, the sun that we still see today. In its time the earth will move: there will be earthquakes. There will be hunger.

The Origin of Music

As the spirits were about to be sacrificed, they gave their cloaks to the people and said, "These are for you. Wear them." But although the cloaks were valuable, the people mourned. They went weeping from one place to another with the cloaks wrapped around their shoulders, asking, "Where are the spirits? Will we never see them again?" Back and forth they traveled, searching everywhere.

One man walked all the way to the eastern ocean, looking for Tezcatlipoca. As he stood on the shore, the spirit appeared to him as triplets, shining in the sky. It said, "Come here, friend. I want you to go to the sun's house and bring back singers and instruments, so that you can make music in memory of me. Call to my three nieces, the whale, the sea turtle, and the sea cow, and tell them to form a bridge across the water."

The man did as he was told and walked over the ocean to the sun's house. As he came close, he saw the sun surrounded by singers dressed in white, red, yellow, and green, playing the skin drum and the log drum.

Looking up, the sun noticed someone approaching and said to his singers, "A thief is here. If he calls out to you, don't answer, because whoever answers him will have to go with him." Then the man called out with a song so sweet they could not resist answering. When he turned to go back, they fell in behind him, bringing their drums, playing and singing as they walked along.

From that time on, people held celebrations and sang songs to honor the spirits. Hearing the music, the spirits would descend from the sky to sing with the people and join in their dances.

Quetzalcoatl in Tula

The first to have many children and become great were the people called Toltecs, long ago in Tula, at a time when Quetzalcoatl was known as their spirit and received their prayers. His temple was there, too, at the top of a high pyramid, so steep and with steps so narrow it had to be climbed on the balls of the feet. Inside, Quetzalcoatl stood draped, always draped with a sheet, for he had the face of a monster. His face was ruined and battered, not human. And his beard, they say, was extremely long and tangled. But Quetzalcoatl was the source of knowledge. All wisdom and abilities flowed from him.

Because the Toltecs were the people of Quetzalcoatl, they had every skill. For them nothing
was difficult. They invented the calendar and gave
names to the different times of the day. They knew
which days were good and which were bad. The
bad were called beast days. If someone had a
dream, the Toltecs could find out what it meant by
looking up the signs and symbols in books called
dream papers.

They knew how to find jade, turquoise, and
other precious stones. In the early morning, when
it was still dark, they would go out to high places
overlooking the countryside. Just as the sun came
up, they would watch to see if any precious stones
were breathing. Perhaps in the distance they would
see a little steam rising from the earth, as if the
earth were smoking. They would go straight to the
spot, and there they would find a large, dull-col-
ored rock, an ordinary rock of no value. This
would be not the jewel itself but only its mother.
Inside the mother, the jewel would be breathing.
Then they would bring it home and crack it open.

The Toltecs were rich. Foods were cheap, and
vegetables grew so tall, they could be climbed like
trees. The squashes, they say, were as round as the
circle of your arms, and ears of corn were so long
and so fat you could hug them. They had choco-

late, and they had cotton in all different colors: red, yellow, rose, violet, green, white, and brown. They never had to dye it. It simply grew that way.

Quetzalcoatl himself led a pure and holy life, pricking the flesh of his shinbone and drawing blood, and in the dead of night he would go to the river and clean himself with cold water. From him

the people learned what it was to be holy and to live like a priest.

But Tezcatlipoca, looking down from the sky, grew jealous. "The people have forgotten me," he thought. Then he collected spider webs and twisted them into a strong rope, tying one end to the clouds and letting the other end fall to earth. Slowly he climbed down the rope, coming closer and closer to the city of Tula.

THE FALL
OF TULA

The King's Daughter
and the Pepper Man

Tezcatlipoca cast a spell and changed himself into a wild man—just walked around with everything hanging out—sold chili peppers, and went and set himself up in the marketplace at the door of the king's palace.

Now, King Huemac had an appetizing daughter, and all the Toltec men desired her, kept asking to marry her, and the king would not listen, would not give her to anyone.

But the daughter came out to take a look at the marketplace, saw the wild man with everything hanging out, and was stricken immediately. She rushed back inside all hot and swollen, desiring the wild man's *tototl.*

When Huemac heard that his daughter was sick, he asked the women who guarded her, "What happened? What was it? Why is my little daughter all swollen?"

"It was a wild man selling chili peppers," said the women. "He made her desire him and now she is burning up. That's how it started. That's why she is sick."

Then the king issued a command, saying, "Toltecs, look for a wild man selling peppers and bring him here."

They looked everywhere, and when they could not find him, the crier shouted from Crying Out Mound, "Toltecs, do you see a wild man selling peppers anywhere? Bring him in! The king wants him!"

They searched, searched all of Tula, and when they had worn themselves out, finding him nowhere, they went and told the king that he could not be found. But at the last moment he reappeared on his own, right where he had been standing before, right where he had first been seen. And when they saw him, they rushed to tell the king that the wild man was back.

"Let him come quickly," said Huemac, and the Toltecs rushed out and seized the wild man and brought him before the king.

When they had brought him in, the king said, "Who are you?"

"I am a savage," he answered, "I sell little chilis."

"And where do you think you are, you savage? Put on a loincloth, cover yourself!" cried the king.

"But this is my custom," said the pepper man.

"Very well," said the king. "But you have upset my daughter. You must cure her."

"That would be improper. You are a great lord, and I am only a pepper man," he said. "It would be better if you had me killed."

"No, you must cure her. Have no fear."

And at the king's command they trimmed his hair, dipped him in water, bathed him, and oiled him. Then they gave him a loincloth and made him wear it.

As soon as he was presentable, the king said,

47

"Here is my daughter. She is yours." With that they were married, and the princess was cured.

But when the people of Tula heard what had happened, they laughed. "The king has married his daughter to a wild man!" they cried.

After a few days, the king called his councilors and said, "The people are mocking me for taking a wild man as my son-in-law. He has to be gotten rid of."

"How can we do it?"

"Take him to war against our enemies at Grass Mountain, and put him in charge of the dwarfs. As soon as the battle starts, leave him, and he'll be killed. That's my plan," said the king.

Immediately a war was declared, and they all marched off to Grass Mountain. When they got to the battlefield, the men of Tula pulled away, leaving the pepper man with all the dwarfs clinging to him. Unafraid, the pepper man shouted words of encouragement to the dwarfs, ordering them to stand their ground.

Meanwhile, the Toltecs were saying to each other, "Before we go home, we'll attack from the rear and take a few Grass Mountain prisoners." But as they tried to attack, the enemy overwhelmed them and sent them running away. When they got

back to Tula, they merely reported to the king that the son-in-law and the dwarfs had been left behind and had no doubt been killed. The king was pleased.

But at Grass Mountain, as the enemy rushed in on all sides, the wild man roared at the dwarfs and made their hearts strong:

"Brothers, move!
Uncles, move!"

In a fury the dwarfs struck back. They pushed and pounded and kicked until the Grass Mountain warriors lay dead in a heap. There were so many they couldn't be counted.

When word of the victory got back to the king, he called for his councilors and said, "I hear great news. We have a victory. Now we must go and greet them with war honors."

As the king strutted into the market square, holding up a quetzal headdress and a turquoise shield, the people cheered and flocked around him. Then they all went out to the edge of the city to meet the returning warriors, proud as lords, dancing, and singing songs of praise. The shell trumpets were booming.

When they had brought the pepper man back to the palace, they crowned him with the headdress, gave him the turquoise shield, and smeared his face and all the dwarfs' faces with yellow paint. Then the king said to the pepper man, "The people's hearts are satisfied. Now you are really our son-in-law. Be received on this soil. Rest your feet."

The Sorcerer's Dance

After Tezcatlipoca had married the king's daughter and beaten the king's enemies, and the people had decorated him with feathers, he arranged to have a dance. To announce it, the crier climbed Crying Out Mound and shouted in all directions. Hearing the call, Toltecs arrived quickly from the countryside.

Maidens and marriageable young men came first, following close behind Tezcatlipoca as he led the way to the edge of a canyon on the outskirts of the city. Because he was a sorcerer, the people immediately did what he wanted without being told. As he struck up the beat with his drum, they started to dance, and while they danced, he composed a song, singing it out loud so that everyone could repeat the words after him.

As they leaped in the air, hand in hand, their singing became a roar that could be heard from far away. This was at night, just after the sun had gone down.

In the dark, as they danced, they bumped each other, pushing first one and then another over the edge of the cliff. Those who fell were killed on the crags below, and as they died they were turned into rocks. Others swarmed over the bridge that crossed the canyon. But though the bridge was of stone, the sorcerer broke it, and all the people fell on the crags. The more they danced, the more they fell. It was as though the dancing had made them drunk.

The next night the Toltecs danced again. Nobody remembered what had happened the night before, and again they leaped and sang and pushed each other over the edge. Night after night they returned to the cliff, the sorcerer drumming and leading the song, and each time they danced more people were killed.

Master Log

Here's another thing that happened. It was in the middle of the market square and the sorcerer had sat down with a tiny man who danced in the palm of his hand. "I'm Master Log," he said, "and this is Huitzilopochtli."

As little Huitzilopochtli danced, the people of Tula fell all over themselves to get a closer look. They pushed and shoved and trampled each other until forty were crushed to death. The next day it happened again, and the day after that. Every day forty were crushed. Finally the sorcerer said, "Toltecs, why do you put up with this? Don't be killed. Look for stones, and stone me."

Without thinking, the people picked up stones and threw them at the sorcerer. They stoned him from all directions, and it wasn't long before he lay dead. But after that he began to stink. The odor was horrible, so strong that people throughout the city fainted, and many died. Wherever the wind carried the stench, people were killed.

At last the dead man opened his mouth and said, "Toltecs, why do you put up with this? Don't be killed. Look for a rope, and haul me away." They found a rope and, without thinking, tied it around the sorcerer's body and began to pull. It was then that they found out how heavy he was, so heavy he couldn't be moved. They had never imagined he could weigh so much. It had never occurred to them. Well, it was time for a cry, so the crier climbed Crying Out Mound and shouted, "Toltecs, bring your heaviest log-hauling ropes and haul the dead man away."

From everywhere they came running, dragging their ropes. They tied them to the sorcerer's body and started to pull, singing, "Toltecs, move. Toltecs, heave." But it wouldn't budge. They pulled harder, and when one of the ropes snapped, all the

men down along the line fell on top of one another
and were killed. Another rope snapped, and more
men were killed. Still they were singing, "Toltecs,
heave. Toltecs, move." But when the same thing
had happened several times, the dead man opened
his mouth and said, "Toltecs, why do you put up
with this? Don't be killed. Give me a song of my
own." And he sang it for them:

> *"Pull our log*
> *Our master*
> *Master Log"*

All together they sang the sorcerer's song, and with that the body began to move. It moved so quickly, sliding along, that whenever the Toltecs stopped to catch their breath, the dead man kept coming and would run them over, killing them by twenties and forties. When at last they had hauled him completely away, the few who were left returned to their homes without remembering what had happened. They had no idea what had been done to them. It was as if they were drunk.

The Flight of Quetzalcoatl

One day the sorcerer became a little old man. Stooped over and white-headed, carrying a bowl of agave wine, he made his way to the temple to pay a call on Quetzalcoatl. When he got to the entrance, he said, "I want to see the master." But the guards told him, "Go away, old man, the master is sick. You will only bother him."

"Oh no," said the little man, "I have to see him."

"Very well," said the guards. "But wait here." Then they went and told the master, "Lord, a little man has come to see you. We tried to send him away, but he refuses to go."

"Let him come in," said Quetzalcoatl. "He is the one I have been expecting for as many days as there are fingers on my two hands."

Then they went back and got him, and when they had brought him before the master, he said, "My grandchild, how are you feeling? Here, I have brought you medicine. Drink it."

"Old one, come close," replied Quetzalcoatl. "Did you travel far? You must be tired, you must be weary. I have been expecting you for as many days as there are fingers on my two hands."

"But, my grandchild, tell me, how are you feeling?"

"I hurt all over," he replied. "I can hardly move my hands and feet."

"Drink this medicine," said the little man. "It will cure you. First it will go to your head and make your body feel better. Then it will work in your heart and make you cry, because it will make you think about death and about going away to a different place."

"What place is that?"

"The place where the sun comes up. When you get there, you will meet the old man who is in charge of things. Then, when you come back, you will be as young as a child."

Quetzalcoatl felt his heart leap. The little man urged him on and said, "Come, drink this medicine." But he would not drink it.

"Taste it. You will like it," said the little man. "Put it in front of you. This is your fortune, your desire. Taste just a little." Quetzalcoatl tasted it, then took a deep drink. "It tastes good," he said, "and it kills the pain. I don't feel sick anymore."

"Take another. It will make you strong." Quetzalcoatl took another, and after that he was drunk. Then he began to cry, pouring out his grief, unable to think of anything but what he had known from the beginning, that the sorcerer had come to trick him.

Then he gathered his servants together and got ready to leave. At his command they set fire to the houses. All the palaces, shining with silver and shell, were burned to the ground. And all the Toltecs' treasures were buried in steep, dangerous places, in mountain ravines and in canyons. He set free all the valuable birds, the quetzals, the cotingas, and the roseate spoonbills. They flew ahead of him as he made his way toward the place where the sun comes up.

Traveling along, he came to a tall tree with spreading branches and a thick trunk. As he stood in front of it, he asked his servants to hand him his mirror. When he looked at himself, he said, "I thought so. Already I am old." Then he named this place Beneath the Old Age Tree, and he picked up stones and threw them at the trunk with so much force that they stuck in the bark until it was all encrusted from top to bottom.

The next thing he came to was a boulder, where he sat down to rest. From there, looking back, he could see Tula, and it made him cry. As the tears dropped from his cheeks, they fell like hailstones, piercing the rock, making two little hollows. The boulder was soft, like mud, so that his haunches sank into it, and so did his hands where he supported his weight. When he got up to leave, the marks were visible, and to this day they can be seen there. Then he named the place Where the Handprints Are.

The third place he came to was Stone Crossing, where there was a wide river. He laid huge rocks in the water to make a bridge, crossed over, and continued on his way, and it is for this reason that the place is called Stone Crossing.

The fourth place was Serpent Spring. When he got there, demons tried to stop him and turn him back. "Where are you going?" they wanted to know.

"To the house of the dawn," he replied. "The sun has called me home."

"Very well," they said. "We cannot stop you. But we will not let you take your jewels. You must leave these behind," and they named all the arts of the Toltecs, the art of casting gold, the art of stonecutting, the art of bookmaking, the art of featherwork, and all the others. Then Quetzalcoatl removed the jewels from around his neck and let them fall into the water. Because of this, he renamed the place Jewel Spring.

The fifth was Sleeping Place, and there another demon came out to meet him. "Where are you going?" he asked.

"To the house of the dawn," he replied. "The sun has called me home."

"Very well," said the demon. "But here, take this. You must drink this wine."

"Oh no," he said, "I won't drink wine. I won't even taste it."

"But you must," said the demon. "I let no one pass who doesn't drink my wine." So Quetzalcoatl took the wine, thinking he would save himself by sipping it through a straw. But the wine overpowered him even so, and he fell to the ground in a stupor and snored so loud it was as if there were thunder. When he awoke, he said, "This will be

called Sleeping Place." Then he looked at himself in his mirror, rearranged his headdress, and went on his way.

As he came out through the high pass between White Woman and Popocatepetl, the snow and ice were so cold that all his servants, who were very small, being dwarfs and hunchbacks, froze to death. At this he wept bitterly, moaning and sighing. Now he was alone as he descended into the countryside.

Traveling on, he stopped at many places, setting up landmarks so that he would be remembered.

One place he slid down a hillside, leaving a scar that can still be seen. Another place he set up a ball court of stone, and the center line was a deep crevice. Another place he uprooted a silk-cotton tree and shot it like an arrow into a second silk-cotton tree, so that the two formed a cross. He also made underground rooms, all of stone, at a place called Mitla. And he set up a huge balanced rock that anyone could tilt with the touch of a finger, but even if many men pushed together, no matter where they stood, they could never tip it over.

And there were many other things he did, and he named all the mountains and all the parts of the different countries he passed through as he made his way to the ocean. When he got to the shore he wove live snakes together to form a boat, settled himself inside it, and disappeared across the water. How he got to the house of the dawn nobody knows.

THE
FOUNDING
OF MEXICO

The Birth of Huitzilopochtli

At Snake Mountain, a day's journey from Tula, there lived a woman named Coatlicue, mother of the four hundred *huitznahua*, whose elder sister was Coyolxauhqui. Coatlicue did holy work. She swept, making everything clean, and that was the holy work she did at Snake Mountain. Once, while Coatlicue was sweeping, a tuft of feathers fell down beside her, and she picked it up and tucked it inside her skirt. When she had finished sweeping, she looked for the feathers but couldn't find them, and after that she became pregnant.

When the four hundred *huitznahua* saw that their mother was going to have a child, they took it as an insult. "Who did this?" they asked each other. "What made her pregnant? It shames us." But the elder sister, Coyolxauhqui, said, "Brothers, what made her pregnant is what is inside her. She herself is the one to blame, and for this we will have to kill her."

Coatlicue was frightened when she learned what they were thinking, but the child inside her comforted her by calling out, "Don't worry, I know what to do," and she seemed to understand what he was saying and it eased her mind.

As the four hundred *huitznahua* talked about killing their mother to get rid of the shame, they braced themselves as if for war. Their elder sister, Coyolxauhqui, stirred up their minds and made them furious, so that there would be no mistake about the mother being killed. Then they dressed as warriors and each wound his hair around his head in a warrior's headdress.

But one of the warriors, named Standing Tree, was a traitor, and he went and told the unborn child, who was Huitzilopochtli, everything the brothers were saying. "Standing Tree, you will be my lookout," said Huitzilopochtli. "Watch them and keep listening to what they say, because I know what to do."

When at last they had made up their minds to kill the mother, they excitedly threw on their war gear, handed out weapons, and put nettles into their paper caps. They tied war bells around their legs; and their spears were sharp as knives. Then, with Coyolxauhqui taking the lead, they all moved out together.

Meanwhile, Standing Tree was running up the mountain to warn Huitzilopochtli.

"They're coming."

"Where, my brother?"

"At the skull rack."

"Where, my brother?"

"At the sand moat."

"Where, my brother?"

"Halfway up the mountain."

"Where, my brother?"

"Here! And Coyolxauhqui takes the lead." Then Huitzilopochtli was born in an instant, carrying his weapons with him, shield, spears, and spear-thrower the color of turquoise, his face painted with child's excrement, and a feather headband from ear to ear. He had feathers on the sole of his left foot, and his arms and thighs were striped with blue.

In his left hand he held a snakehead scepter. "Light my scepter," he shouted, and a warrior named Tochancalqui obeyed his command. With the burning scepter he stabbed the elder sister and

cut off her head, so that her body crashed to the
ground, breaking to pieces. Her arms and legs fell
in every direction, and what was left of her rolled
all the way to the bottom of the slope. Meanwhile
Huitzilopochtli was charging after the others,

breaking through their ranks, knocking them over,
scattering them off the top of the mountain. And
when they got to the bottom, he chased them
again and made them run in circles; four times he

made them run around the base of Snake Mountain.

In vain they cried for mercy, slapping themselves with their shields. There was nothing more they could do. They were powerless to surround him, and so he routed them, killed them, knocked them dead. And still he wouldn't let them alone, kept grabbing them until they pleaded with him, "Enough!" And even then he would not calm down but drove himself on and kept pursuing them. Only a few got away, and those who did went toward the south, which is called *huitztlampa* because that was the direction taken by the *huitznahua*, or at least by those few who escaped.

When his rage had passed, Huitzilopochtli picked the paper caps off the dead men and placed one of them on his own head. "From now on," he said, "this will be my crown." What's more, Huitzilopochtli was called Awesome, because his mother had been made pregnant by nothing more than a few feathers, and no one seemed to be his father. The Mexicans worshipped him, making sacrifices to him, strengthening him with their prayers. This is the way it was always done, and the origin of it was at Snake Mountain.

That's all there is.

Copil's Heart

As the Mexicans traveled south, not knowing where to build their city, stopping first one place and then another, they had as their elder sister a

woman named Malinalxochitl, who was beautiful and mild-mannered but wise in magic and could kill a man just by looking at him, secretly eating his heart while he was still alive. Or, just at a glance, she could eat the calf of a person's leg without his feeling the pain. Or sometimes she would twist a man's eyesight so that he thought he was seeing an enormous beast or some other terrifying thing. To say it simply, she was the kind of witch known in later times as a heart biter, a calf snatcher, and an eye twister.

There was more. At night, when people were asleep, she would pick up a man and carry him outside the camp and drop him in front of a poisonous snake. Scorpions, centipedes, and spiders were also used by her in her evil work, and, being a witch, she could transform herself into whatever bird or animal she wished. With all her dangerous powers she insisted on being worshipped as a goddess, and no one dared treat her otherwise.

For a while the people put up with this way of life because Malinalxochitl was a sister of the god Huitzilopochtli. But finally, in their prayers, the priests complained to Huitzilopochtli, and he, as was his custom, answered them in their dreams.

"My sister is a menace," he said, "and you must have nothing more to do with her and her enchantments. Tomorrow night, during the first sleep, you will steal away and leave her behind. My charge and destiny is to rule not by witchcraft but by force of arms, arrow and shield, chest and shoulders.

"My orders will be carried out in countries everywhere, and I will stand guard at distant borders to protect the people, seeing that they live well, glorifying the name of the Mexican nation, lifting it to the clouds. Our conquests will bring jade, gold, and colored feathers to decorate my temple, also corn and chocolate of different kinds and cotton of different colors. I will have it all."

The next night, during the first sleep, the people

quietly moved away, leaving Malinalxochitl alone in the woods with only a few servants. When she awoke in the morning, she looked around and began to wail. "My brother has cheated us," she cried. "He has left without a trace and taken his whole hateful pack with him. What can they be thinking of? Where will they settle? The countryside is already filled with people who don't know us and who have armies." Then she and her followers went into the nearest town and pleaded with the town dwellers until she was given permission to settle at a place just outside, called Craggy Hill, afterward called Malinalco, and to this day the people of Malinalco are known to be sorcerers.

Meanwhile the Mexicans continued their march, stopping long enough to plant and harvest a little corn but always moving on, searching for a place to found their city. Eventually they reached the hill of Chapultepec on the shore of the great lake that one day would be known as the Lake of Mexico. But here, more than anywhere else, they found themselves surrounded by strange nations who wished them ill and were only waiting for bad luck to catch up with them.

During these years Malinalxochitl had given birth to a son, who was called Copil, and at last, now that he was fully grown, she could teach him her arts of sorcery and explain to him how her brother, Huitzilopochtli, had turned against her, and the Mexicans had left her sleeping in the woods. Moved by her tears, Copil vowed to seek revenge, using the evil methods she herself had taught him. And as soon as he heard that the Mexicans had camped at Chapultepec, he set out to visit the nearby cities to warn them against their new neighbors.

"Beware the Mexicans," he would say. "They are here to conquer you, and when they have made you their slaves you will come to know their horrible and perverted customs, which I have seen with my own eyes."

In short order the nations of Azcapotzalco, Tlacopan, Coyohuacan, Xochimilco, Chalco, and Colhuacan had formed an alliance and were marching against Chapultepec, while Copil himself climbed a nearby hill to enjoy a better view of the destruction. But before the attack could begin, Huitzilopochtli, who knew everything, instructed his priests to slip up behind Copil, seize him, and cut out his heart. When they had done so, and the heart had been presented to Huitzilopochtli, he ordered them to take it into the lake and throw it as far as possible. Without delay, one of the priests waded into the water and, throwing the heart with all his strength, saw it fall on a marshy island; and it is said that from Copil's heart sprang the prickly pear that marked the future site of the city of Mexico.

The Woman of Discord

After the Mexicans had been defeated at Chapultepec, those who escaped with their lives fled to the south shore of the great lake and begged the king of Colhuacan, who ruled the countryside there, to give them a place to camp. Thinking he would soon be rid of them, the king cunningly invited them to settle at an uninhabited spot called Chalk Water, and they, with thanks, moved off to build their huts and plant their fields.

Arriving at Chalk Water, they found it infested with snakes and insects so deadly that they feared for their lives. But Huitzilopochtli spoke to them in dreams, showing them how to catch and tame the poisonous creatures and turn them into a tasty dish; and after many days, when the king's messengers arrived to see if any Mexicans were still alive, they were amazed to find houses and even a small temple, and the fields well cultivated, and the spits and the ollas loaded with snakes, some roasted, some boiled.

When the news got back to the king, he began to respect the Mexicans, thinking, "These people are greatly favored by their god." After that, they were allowed to come into the city of Colhuacan to trade, and before long they were intermarrying with the king's people.

But Huitzilopochtli disliked this friendship with Colhuacan that did nothing but postpone the day when Mexicans would be masters in their own home. So he called out to his priests, "We must have a woman who will be known as the woman of discord, to be worshipped as Our Grandmother

when we have built our city. We must move away
from this place, and we must show the world that
we have bows and arrows, shields and swords. Prepare your weapons, then give Colhuacan a reason

77

for war. Do this: go to their king and ask for his daughter to serve me as my priestess. He will give her to you, and she will become the woman of discord, as you will see."

Never failing to obey Huitzilopochtli, the Mexicans went and asked the king for his daughter, promising to make her their queen and the wife of their god. The greedy king, seizing the opportunity to have his daughter become both queen and goddess, gave permission at once, and they carried her off with pomp and rejoicing.

That night Huitzilopochtli appeared to his priests and said, "I told you this woman would be the cause for war. Now you must make my prediction come true. You must sacrifice her in my honor, and from this day on I will call her my grandmother. Flay her, dress a young boy in her skin, and have him put on her girl's clothing. When all is ready, go tell the king to come worship."

Always obedient, the Mexicans did as their god commanded, and when the king arrived with his retinue of nobles and warriors, the priests invited him to enter a darkened chamber to make offerings to his daughter, the goddess. At first the king could see nothing and began dutifully laying out flowers and twisting the necks of quail. But when he touched fire to the incense he had brought, and the flame shot upward, he immediately saw what had been done to his daughter. He dropped the incense burner and ran from the room, shouting, "Come look, men of Colhuacan. They have murdered my daughter and dressed a boy in her skin. Put an end to them, kill them, erase their name!"

Hearing the king's cries, the Mexicans threw their hands on their weapons and, gathering their women and children, faced their attackers at the lake shore, protected from behind by the water. More warriors came quickly from Colhuacan, and the king's men drove the Mexicans deeper and deeper into the mud. But, stirred by the cries of their women, the Mexicans broke through the enemy's ranks, regained dry ground, and fled along the shore. When at last they had outdistanced the king's army, they threw their shields on the water, climbed onto them, men, women, and children, and rowed as swiftly as possible to the marshy islands in the middle of the lake. There, among the reeds, cold and miserable, they huddled in silence until the danger passed.

The Eagle
on the Prickly Pear

Having escaped from Colhuacan, the Mexicans began wandering over the marshy islands in the
middle of the lake, stopping briefly at a spot where
one of their daughters, Corn Blossom, gave birth
to a baby called Jug Boy, and the place is still
known as Childbirth.

At another place they stopped to build a sweat
bath for Corn Blossom, the mother of Jug Boy, and
gave it the name Bath. Then all the Mexicans
took baths and camped for a while. From there two
elders, Cuauhcoatl and the priest Axolohua, went
into the reeds to a spot now known as Reeds and
Rushes, hunting for a place to settle permanently;
and here they saw a great many wonderful things,
all of which had been predicted by Huitzilopochtli,
who had told them exactly what they would find.
This spot, he had said, would be his fortress and
his home. Suddenly they saw that the cypress trees
were white.

And the willow trees were white.

And the reeds were white.

And the rushes were white.

And the frogs that lived in the water were
white.

And the fish were white.

And the snakes were white.

And just ahead they saw a jumble of crags and caverns, and those that lay to the east were the ones called Fire Water and Water Burn. Those on the north, all jumbled, were the ones called Blue Water and Parrot-colored Water. When they saw all this, they wept.

"Here must be the place," they cried. "Now we have seen what our god was telling us about when he sent us on our way and said, 'In the reeds you will see many things.' Now we have seen them and his words have come true. Let us go back to camp and wait for him to tell us what will happen next."

That night Huitzilopochtli appeared to Cuauh-coatl in a dream, saying, "Cuauhcoatl, you have seen everything that was in the reeds. But listen, there is something more you haven't seen, and I want you to go find it. It is a prickly pear, and on top of it you will see an eagle, contentedly eating, and sunning himself. You will be pleased because it comes from Copil's heart. You were the one who threw it from the shore when we were at Chap-ultepec. It fell beside the crags at Reeds and Rushes and began to grow, and now it is called *tenochtli.* It is where our home and our fortress will be, where we will wait for intruders and meet them with chest and shoulders, arrow and shield.

"This is Mexico, this is Tenochtitlan, where the eagle screams, spreads his wings, and eats, where the fish flies, where the snake rustles.

"This is Mexico, this is Tenochtitlan. And many things will be done."

"Your heart is generous," said Cuauhcoatl. "Now all the elders must hear what you have told me," and the next day he called the Mexicans to-gether and revealed his dream. Immediately they returned to the edge of the caverns at Reeds and Rushes, and as they passed through the reeds, there in front of them was the prickly pear with the eagle perched on top, contentedly eating, his claws punching holes in his prey. When he saw the Mexicans in the distance, he bowed to them.

The eagle's nest was all of precious feathers, cotinga and roseate spoonbill, and there were quetzal plumes. Scattered around were the heads, claws, and bones of the different birds the eagle had killed.

The voice of the spirit said, "Mexicans, this is the place." And with that they all wept. "We are favored," they said. "We are blessed. We have seen where our city will be. Now let us go rest."

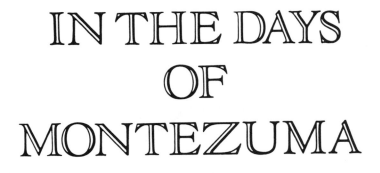

IN THE DAYS
OF
MONTEZUMA

The Talking Stone

Montezuma loved nothing more than to order great monuments that would make him famous. Beautiful things, it was true, had been commissioned by the kings who had gone before, but to Montezuma those works were insignificant. "Not splendid enough for Mexico," he would say, and as the years went by he grew to have doubts about even the huge round-stone where prisoners were sacrificed to Huitzilopochtli. "I want a new one," he said at last, "and I want it a forearm wider and two forearms taller."

So the order went out to the stonecutters to search the countryside for a boulder that could be carved into a round-stone a forearm wider and two forearms taller. When the proper stone had been sighted, at a place called Acolco, haulers and lift-

ers were summoned from six cities and told to bring ropes and levers. Using their levers, they pried the stone from the hillside and dragged it to a level spot to be carved. As soon as it was in position, thirty stonecutters began to chisel it with their flint chisels, making it not only bigger than any round-stone that had been seen before, but more unusual and more beautiful. During the time that they worked, they ate only the rarest delicacies, sent by Montezuma and served by the people of Acolco.

When the stone was ready to be taken to Mexico, the carvers sent word to the king, who ordered the temple priests to go bring incense and a supply of quails. Arriving at the stone, the priests decorated it with paper streamers, perfumed it with the incense, and spattered molten rubber. Then they twisted the necks of the quails and spattered quail blood. There were musicians, too, with conch horns and skin drums. And comedians also came, so that the stone could be entertained as it traveled along.

But when they tried to pull it, it would not be moved. It seemed to have grown roots, and all the ropes snapped as if they had been cotton threads. Two more cities were ordered to send haulers, and as they set to work, shouting back and forth, trussing it with fresh ropes, the stone spoke up and said, "Try what you will."

Suddenly the shouting stopped. "Why do you pull me?" said the stone. "I am not about to turn over and go, I am not to be pulled where you want me to go."

Quietly the men kept working. "Then pull me," it said. "I'll talk to you later." And with that the stone slid forward, traveling easily as far as Tlapitzahuayan. There the haulers decided to rest for the day, while two stonecutters went ahead to warn Montezuma that the great stone had begun to talk.

"Are you drunk?" said the king when they gave

him the news. "Why come here telling me lies?"
Then he called for his storekeeper and had the two
messengers locked up. But he sent six lords to find
out the truth, and when they had heard the stone

say, "Try what you will, I am not to be pulled,"
they went back to Mexico and reported it to Montezuma, and the two prisoners were set free.

In the morning the stone spoke again. "Will you
never understand? Why do you pull me? I am not
to be taken to Mexico. Tell Montezuma it is no
use. The time is bad, and his end is near. He has
tried to make himself greater than our lord who

created the sky and the earth. But pull me if you must, you poor ones. Let's go." And with that the stone slid along until it reached Itztapalapan.

Again it halted, and again they sent messengers to tell Montezuma what it had said. Just as before, he flew into a rage, but this time he was secretly frightened, and although he refused to give the messengers credit for bringing him the truth, he stopped short of jailing them and told them to go back and carry out his orders.

The next morning, as the haulers picked up their ropes, they found that the stone once again moved easily, sliding as far as the causeway that led to Mexico. Advised that the stone had reached the other side of the water, Montezuma sent priests to greet it with flowers and incense, also to appease it with blood sacrifices in case it might be angry. Again it started to move. But when it was halfway across the lake, it stopped and said, "Here and no farther," and although the causeway was made of cedar beams seven hands thick, the stone broke through them, crashing into the water with a noise like thunder. All the men who were tied to the ropes were dragged down and killed, and many others were wounded.

Told what had happened, Montezuma himself

came onto the causeway to see where the stone had disappeared. Still thinking he would carry out his plan, he ordered divers to search the bottom of the lake to see if the stone had settled in a place where it might be hauled back to dry land. But they could find neither the stone itself nor any sign of the men who had been killed. The divers were sent down a second time, and when they came back up they said, "Lord, we see a narrow trace in the water leading toward Acolco."

"Very well," said Montezuma, and with no further questioning he sent his stonecutters back to Acolco to see what they might discover, and when they returned, they reported no more than what the king already knew. Still tied with its ropes and spattered with incense and blood offerings, the stone had gone back to the hillside where it had originally been found.

Then Montezuma turned to his lords and said, "Brothers, I know now that our pains and troubles will be many and our days will be few. As for me, just as with the kings that have gone before, I must let myself die. May the Lord of Creation do what he pleases."

Montezuma's Wound

Near the town of Coatepec in the province of Tex-coco, a poor man was digging in his garden one day when an eagle swooped out of the air, seized him by the scalp, and carried him up toward the clouds, higher and higher, until the two of them were only a speck in the sky that quickly disappeared. Reaching a mountain peak, the man was taken into a dark cavern, where he heard the eagle say, "Lord of all power, I have carried out your command and here is the poor farmer you told me to bring."

Without seeing who spoke, the man heard a voice say, "It is good. Bring him here," and without knowing who took his hand, he found himself being led into a dazzling chamber, where he saw King Montezuma lying unconscious, as if asleep. The man was told to sit next to the king, flowers were put in his hand, and he was given a smoking tube filled with tobacco.

"Here, take these and relax," he was told, "and look carefully at this miserable one who feels nothing. He is so drunk with pride that he closes his eyes to the whole world, and if you want to know how far it has carried him, hold your lighted smok-

ing tube against his thigh and you will see that he
doesn't feel it."

Afraid to touch the king, the poor farmer hesi-
tated. "Do it!" he was commanded. Then he held
the hot tip of the tobacco against the king's thigh
and saw that he felt nothing. He did not even stir.

The voice continued. "You see how drunk he is
with his own power. It is for this reason that I had
you brought here. Now go back where you came

from and tell Montezuma what you have seen and what I ordered you to do. So that he will believe you, have him show you his thigh. Then point to the spot where you touched him and he will find a burn. Tell him that the Lord of Creation is angry and that because of his arrogance his rule is about to end. The time is short. Say to him, 'Enjoy what is left!'"

With those words the eagle reappeared, took hold of the man's scalp, and carried him back to his garden. As it turned to leave, it said, "Listen to me, poor farmer. Don't be afraid. Strengthen your heart and do what the lord commands, not forgetting a single word that he told you to say." Then the bird rose into the air and vanished.

The poor farmer stood amazed, but with his digging stick still in his hand he went straight to Mexico and asked to speak to Montezuma. Given permission to enter, he bowed low and said, "Lord, I come from Coatepec, and while I was working in my garden an eagle came and took me to a place where there was a lord of great power. He made me sit down where it was bright and shining, and you were there beside me. Then he gave me flowers and a lighted smoking tube, and when it got hot he commanded me to hold it against your thigh. I burned you with it, but you felt nothing and didn't move. He told me you didn't know what was happening because of your pride, and very soon your rule would come to an end and you would be in trouble, because your deeds are not good. Then he told me to come back and tell you what I saw. The time will be short. Enjoy what is left."

Remembering a dream he had had the night before, in which a poor man had wounded him with a smoking tube, Montezuma looked down at his thigh and saw that he had been burned. Suddenly the wound was so painful that he could not touch it. Without a word to the poor farmer, he called for his storekeeper and ordered him to lock the man up and give him no food until he died of starvation. As the prisoner was being led away, the pain increased and Montezuma himself had to be taken to his bed. For four days he lay suffering, and only with great difficulty were his doctors able to make him well.

Eight Omens

Ten years before the Spaniards arrived, the sky omen appeared for the first time. It was like a fire tassel, a fire plume, a shower of dawn light that pierced the sky, narrow at the tip, wide at the base. Rising in the east, it reached all the way to the sky's center, the heart of the sky, right to the sky's heart, and so bright when it came up that it seemed like daybreak in the middle of night. Then at sunrise, it would disappear. It began in 12 House and kept coming up for a whole year. As soon as it appeared, men cried out, slapping their mouths with the palms of their hands. Everybody was afraid, everybody wailed.

There was a second omen here in Mexico. A fire broke out in the house of the devil Huitzilopochtli, the house known as His Kind of Mountain at the place called Commander's. Nobody set it. It flared on its own. When it was first noticed, the wooden pillars were already burning, and the fire tassels, the fire tongues, the fire plumes were shooting out, licking the whole temple. People were screaming. They said, "Mexicans, your water jars! Run! Put it out!" But when they poured water, it just fanned the flames, and then there was a real fire.

A third omen. The thatch-roofed temple of the fire god, the temple called Tzommolco, was hit by lightning. It was considered an omen because there was no heavy rain, just a sprinkle. It was a heat flash for no reason. There was no thunder.

A fourth omen. While it was still daylight, a comet that looked like three comets came out of the west and fell in the east, like a long-tailed shower of sparks, with its tail stretched out far. As soon as it was seen, there was a great roar, as though people were screaming everywhere.

A fifth omen. The lake boiled without any wind to make it boil. It sort of welled up, welled up swirling. And when it rose, it went very far, all the way to the bottoms of the houses, flooding them. Houses were crumbling. This was the big lake next to us here in Mexico.

A sixth omen. Often a woman was heard. She went weeping and crying. At night she cried out loud and said, "My children, already we're passing away." Sometimes she said, "My children, where can I take you?"

A seventh omen. One day when the water people were hunting, using their snares, they caught an ash-colored bird like a crane, and they brought it to the Black Chambers to show it to Montezuma. The sun had peaked, but it was still daylight. On the bird's head was a kind of mirror, a kind of reflecting surface, round and circular, and in it you could observe the sky and the constellation Fire Drill. When Montezuma saw this, he took it as a great omen. And when he looked again, he saw what seemed to be people coming into view, coming as conquerors with weapons, riding on animals. Then he called his astrologers and wise men and said, "Do you see what I see? It looks like people coming into view." But as they were about to answer him, the image disappeared and they could tell him nothing.

An eighth omen. Monstrous people kept showing up with two heads on one body. They were

taken to the Black Chambers for Montezuma to see, but as soon as he looked at them, they disappeared.

The Return of Quetzalcoatl

One day a poor man who had no ears, no thumbs, and no big toes came before Montezuma and explained that he had something to tell. Wondering what kind of creature this could be, Montezuma

99

asked where he had come from. "From Deadland Woods," was the reply. And who had sent him? He had come on his own to serve the king and to tell what he had seen. He had been walking along the ocean, he said, when he had noticed what seemed to be a large hill moving from one place to another on the water, and no such thing had ever been seen before.

"Very well," said Montezuma. "Rest yourself, catch your breath." Then he called for his storekeeper and told him to lock the man up and watch him carefully.

As the prisoner was being taken away, the king ordered his chief server, Tlillancalqui, to leave immediately for the seacoast to find out if the man with no thumbs had been telling the truth. "Take along your slave Girded Loins. Go to the ruler who serves me in Cuetlaxtlan and speak harshly to him. Say, 'Who stands guard here? Is there something on the ocean? Why hasn't the king been told, and what is it?'"

When they got to Cuetlaxtlan, they asked for the ruler and gave him the king's message word for word. "Sit down and rest," said the ruler. Then he sent a runner along the shore to find out the truth, and when the man returned, he was running fast.

"I see something like two pyramids or a pair of hills," he said, "and it moves on top of the water."

The chief server and Girded Loins went to look for themselves. They saw the thing moving not far from the beach, and there were seven or eight men who came out in a little boat, fishing with fish-hooks. To get a better view, they climbed a white-wood tree, a very bushy one, and watched until the fishermen returned to the twin pyramids with their catch. Then the chief server said, "Girded Loins, let's go," and they climbed out of the tree, went back to Cuetlaxtlan to pay their respects to the ruler, and rushed home to Mexico Tenoch-titlan.

When they reached the city, they went directly to the palace to tell Montezuma what had been seen. "Lord and king, it is true. An unknown kind of people has come to the edge of the ocean, and we saw them fishing from a boat, some with poles, some with nets. When they had made their catch, they went back to the two pyramids that float on the water and were carried up into them. There may be fifteen in all, dressed in different colors, blue, brown, green, dirty gray, and red. They have headdresses like cooking pots that must be for pro-tection against the sun. Their skin is very light,

101

lighter than ours, but most have long beards, and their hair hangs only to their ears."

At this news Montezuma bowed his head and, without saying a word, put his hand on his mouth and sat motionless for a long time, as though he were dead or dumb, powerless to speak. At last he said, "Who can I trust if not you, a lord in my palace? You bring me the truth every day." Then he told his storekeeper to go get the man with no thumbs and set him free. But when they went to the locker and opened the door, the man wasn't there. He had disappeared.

The storekeeper was amazed and ran to tell Montezuma, who was also amazed, but after a moment's thought said, "No, I am not surprised, because almost all those people from the coast are wizards." And then he said, "Now I will give you an order that you must keep secret on pain of death. If you reveal it to anyone, I will have to bury you beneath my chair, and all your wives and children will be put to death and everything you have will be taken away and all your houses torn down and their foundations dug up until the water spurts from the ground. Secretly, then, I want you to bring me the two best gold casters, the two best jade carvers, and the two best feather workers," and without delay the storekeeper went and found them. "Lord, they are here," he called.

"Show them in," answered the king, and when he saw them he said, "My fathers, you have been brought for a particular purpose. Reveal it to any man and you will suffer death and all penalties, houses uprooted, loss of possessions, and death to your wives, children, and relatives. Now, each of you must make two works. There must be a gold neck chain, each link four fingers wide, with pendants and medals; and gold wristbands, ear jewels, and lip plugs all of the finest design; and two great fans, one with a gold half-moon in the center and the other with a polished gold sun that can be seen from far away. You must do it as quickly as possible."

In only a few days and nights the work was finished, and in the morning, when Montezuma was awake, they sent one of his dwarfs to tell him to come to the hall of the birds to see what had been made. "My lord, examine it," they said when they saw him coming, and when he examined it, he found it good. He called for his storekeeper and said, "Take these grandfathers of mine and give them each a load of coarse mantles of four, eight, and ten forearms mixed, also fine mantles, blouses, and skirts for my grandmothers, and corn, chilis, squash seeds, cotton, and beans," and with these things the workers went home contented.

Montezuma then showed the jewels and the featherwork to his chief server and said, "Here, the gifts are finished. You must take them to the one who has arrived, the one we have been expecting. I am convinced it is the spirit Quetzalcoatl. When he went away, he promised to come back and rule in Tula and in all the world. The old people of Tula are certain of this. And before he left, he buried his treasure in mountain ravines and in canyons, and these are the gold and precious stones we find today. Since it is known that he would return from the place in the sky beyond the ocean, the place called House of Dawn, where he went to meet with another spirit, and since it is certain that all kinds of jewels in this world were once part of his treasure, it can only be that he now returns to enjoy what is his. Even this throne is his, and I am only borrowing it.

"Return immediately to Cuetlaxtlan and have the ruler make up all kinds of dishes, tamales, rolled tamales, tortillas with and without beans, all kinds of grilled birds, quail, grilled deer, rabbit, chili powder, stewed greens, and every kind of fruit.

"If you see that he eats these things, you will know he is Quetzalcoatl. If he does not eat them, you will know it is not he. If he likes only human flesh and if he eats you, all will be well because I myself will protect and maintain your houses, your women, and your children forever. Have no fear of it. Take Girded Loins with you, and if you see by these signs that their lord is Quetzalcoatl, adorn him with the jewels and give him the two large fans. Humbly beg him to let me die, and when I am dead he may come enjoy his mat and throne, which I have been guarding for him."

The next morning the chief server and Girded Loins set out with the gifts, traveling day and night. The moment they reached Cuetlaxtlan they told the ruler to prepare the food, using the finest ollas and baskets, and at midnight they carried it all to the edge of the ocean, so that at daybreak there they were, waving their arms and signaling across the water.

The small boat was lowered. Four men came rowing to shore to greet them and to ask who they were and where they were from. But the Mexicans answered them only in signs, saying they wished to be taken to their lord to give him the things they had brought. Then they loaded the food and the sacks with the gifts and rowed back across.

105

When they reached the ship, the captain appeared with the Indian woman, Malintzin, who translated his words. "Come here," she said. "Where are you from?"

"We are from the great city of Mexico Tenochtitlan."

"Why do you come here?"

"O lady, our daughter, we have come to see your lord."

Then Malintzin withdrew to an inner room and spoke to the captain. When she reappeared, she asked, "Who is your king?"

"Lady, his name is Montezuma."

"Why did he send you? What did he say?"

"He wants to know where this lord intends to go."

"This lord is your spirit, and he says he will go see King Montezuma."

"That would please him very much. But he begs this lord to let him finish his reign, waiting until after his death before ruling the country he left when he went away."

Then the Mexicans opened their sacks and presented the jeweled gifts and the two great fans, and when these had been received by the captain, they were passed from hand to hand, and the Spaniards admired them with much joy and great satisfaction. "O lady and daughter," said the Mexicans, "we have also brought food for the lord and chocolate for him to drink."

"The spirit will eat this food," said Malintzin, "but first he must see you eat from it yourselves." When the Mexicans had done as they were asked, the Spaniards all ate, offering the chief server and Girded Loins some sea biscuits, which were a little stale, and wine that made them drunk. They said that they wished to return with an answer to their lord Montezuma. "What is your name?" asked Malintzin. "My name is Tlillancalqui," said the chief server. Then she gave him this answer: "Tell Montezuma we kiss his hands and will be back in eight days and come see him."

Carrying these words, the Mexicans returned to their king and reported everything that had happened, describing the weapons they had seen and the horses, and showing him one of the biscuits.

"What flavor does it have?" asked the king, and touching it, he declared that it felt like tufa stone. He called for a piece of tufa, compared it, and found that the biscuit was heavier. Then he called for his dwarfs and ordered them to try it, and though they said it was good-tasting, Montezuma was afraid to eat it himself, saying that this was the food of gods. Instead, he ordered his priests to bring it to Tula and bury it in the temple of Quetzalcoatl. They took the biscuit, placed it in a fine jar all worked with gold, and covered the jar with a cloth. As they traveled north from Mexico, carrying incense burners, they sang songs of Quetzalcoatl, and when they reached Tula, they buried the spirit's food to the sound of shell trumpets, the roaring of conch horns.

"Is It You?"

When the Spaniards arrived at the edge of the city, things came to a head, and it reached the point where Montezuma fixed himself and got dressed up to meet them, along with the other high lords and princes who were his chiefs and nobles. And so they all went out to make the greeting.

Fine flowers were placed on a gourd tray, with popcorn-, yellow tobacco-, and cacao flowers surrounded by shield- and heartflowers in wreaths and garlands, and they brought gold necklaces, collars, and neck bands, so that when Montezuma met them there at Hummingbird Point he had gifts for the captains and warlords. Then he gave them the flowers, necklaced them with necklaces, with

flower necklaces, adorned them with flowers, and wreathed their heads. Then he showed the Marquis all the necklaces made of gold, and as he necklaced him with a few of them, the greeting came to a close.

Then the Marquis said to Montezuma, "Is it you? Are you he? Are you Montezuma?"

"Yes, I am he," said Montezuma, and he arose and went over to him and made a low bow. Then he pulled himself up to his full height, stood straight, and addressed him, saying, "My lord, you must be tired, you must be weary. You have arrived in this city of Mexico. You have reached this mat and throne of yours that I have held for you briefly. I have been taking care of things for you.

Gone are those rulers of yours, Itzcoatl, Montezuma the Elder, Axayacatl, Tizoc, and Ahuitzotl, who briefly stood guard for you, governing this city of Mexico. I, your servant, came after them. I wonder, can they look back and see over their shoulders? If only just one of them could see what I see, could marvel at what is happening to me now! For this is no dream. I am not sleepwalking, not seeing things in my sleep. I am not dreaming that I see you and look into your face. Indeed, I have been troubled for as many days as there are fingers on my two hands. I have gazed into the Unknown and have seen you coming out of the clouds, out of the mists.

Those kings used to say that you would come back to your city and proceed to your mat and throne, that you would return. And this has come true. You are here, and you must be tired, you

must be weary. Welcome to this land. Rest yourself. Go to your palace and rest your body. Our
lords are welcome here."

AFTER
CORTÉS

How the World Began
by Francisco Plácido, 1565

God says it, and he creates it: first was the light.
And on the second day he made the sky.

The third day he makes the ocean and also the
land. And the fourth day he establishes the sun.
Oh, and the moon and all the stars.

On the fifth day the water creatures were made,
then all the birds that fly along.

The sixth day our Lord made the wild beasts and
all the living things on earth, and at that time he
created the first man. "Ah, let it be thus. Our very
likeness, our very image, shall be made. This is the
one that will rule the earth.

"My creation, all that lies on earth, will be his
property and his dominion."

When God had created the first people, then he

blessed them. He says, "Increase, multiply! Dwell in all the earth!

"Behold, for I have given you every fruitful tree that exists in this world and every green herb that is here. Dwell in all the earth!"

For the briefest of moments did they assume the mat and throne of God the Only Spirit. And then the Lord frowns and says, "Adam! O Adam, mark this well. You will get your food on earth with sweat."

And it is said that he expelled them. "When I

say it and require it, then your life will finish here, for truly you are earth, and again you shall be earth."

As people on earth were scattered and sown, they multiplied. And many were the sins. Because of these, indeed a second time God grew angry. He flooded the world.

The mere eight people who were left, the children of Noah, were the ones who reproduced. Truly they found favor. But does our Lord have a mind to frown? Indeed he is provoked!

But ah! Four thousand and three years went by, and God was compassionate: he sent his precious son, the savior.

Through Saint Mary he came to take his precious incarnation. Through his precious death he came to save us, and he gave us everlasting life.

Calling the Ghost of Montezuma
Anonymous, about 1565?

At Flower House of Paintings, in the Flower House of Butterflies, yonder in your home, and as a song you're born, O Montezuma: as a flower you come to bloom on earth, come to give pleasure here beside the drum.

You assemble them all, all your swans. Yonder in your home these butterflies, these hummingbirds, are sipping: now let them live in pleasure here beside the drum.

I marvel at these sky dwellers, these angels. There's flower-singing, jade gongs are ringing in the home of God.

They're loosening their songs: they're entertaining God, bringing down a multitude of flowers. And with these the city, Mexico, is spreading fragrance. Here!

The Virgin of Guadalupe
by Luis Lasso de la Vega, 1649

Ten years after the city of Mexico had been conquered and the shields and arrows had been laid aside and all the towns were at peace, faith and the knowledge of Life Giver, the true spirit, God, were beginning to catch fire and shine. It was early December in the year 1531 and there was a poor man named Juan Diego who lived some distance away in Cuauhtitlan, but at that time everyone still belonged to the church in Tlatelolco and so he was coming in to have religious instruction and to run some errands, very early one Saturday morning.

As he approached the hill called Tepeyacac, just at dawn, he heard music, as if beautiful birds of different kinds were singing on top of the hill, and their throats rang out as though mountains were echoing them, singing even more beautifully than bellbirds or trogons. "Am I worthy of hearing this?" he wondered. "Is this a dream? Am I sleepwalking? Our ancestors used to speak of a flower land in the sky. Am I there?"

As he gazed eastward toward the hilltop, listening to the precious sky music, the singing became suddenly quieter and he heard a voice calling,

"Juanito, Juan Diego." Filled with joy but a little stunned, he dared to climb the hill, and when he reached the top he saw a lady, calling him to come closer. She was wonderfully beautiful, and her dress was glowing like the sun. Her radiance even pierced the rock she stood on, so that it seemed as bright as a jadestone bracelet, and there was rainbow shine all over the ground. As he bowed before her, he heard her lovely voice saying, "Juanito, my child, where are you going?"

"O lady, O virgin," he answered, "I am on my way to your house in Mexico Tlatelolco. The priests are teaching us about religion. They speak for the master, Our Lord."

She said, "Listen carefully, my child. I am the virgin, Saint Mary, mother of the true spirit, Life Giver, Creator, Sky Owner, Earth Owner. I want a church to be built for me, and in this church I will give all my love, all my help, and all my protection. Go to the bishop's palace in Mexico and tell him I have sent you to ask that my church be built on the plain beneath this hill. Child, you have heard my breath and word. Now go."

Arriving in Mexico, he went straight to the palace of the bishop, who was Don Fray Juan de Zumárraga of the Order of Saint Francis. After pleading with the bishop's servants, he was allowed

to enter, and when he went in, he made a low bow
and explained the message he had been given by
the sky lady. He also described everything he had
seen and heard. But when he had finished, the
bishop did not seem convinced. He said, "My son,
you must come some other time and I will listen to
you once more and consider it all over again."

And so his errand was not successful, and he
came away sad. On the way home, as he passed the
hilltop, he found the sky lady waiting for him. "O
virgin," he said, "I did as you asked, and the
bishop was kind to me. But the way he answered, I
knew that his heart was not touched. I could tell
he thought the church was my own idea, not
yours. I beg you to send one of the nobles, someone important who will be believed. I am only a
poor man, and I don't know how to act in the
presence of a bishop. Please pardon me for trou-
bling you. I am afraid I have made you angry."

"My child," said the lady, "you must understand
that there are many people who could be my messengers, but you are the one I have chosen, and
through you my command will be carried out. Go
back to the bishop and tell him again that the one
who sends you is the virgin, Saint Mary, mother of
the spirit God."

The next day, Sunday, Juan Diego left home

early and came straight to Tlatelolco for church services. About ten o'clock, when mass was over and the head count had been completed, he went to the bishop's and again, with great difficulty, managed to see him. This time the bishop said, "It is not enough that you bring me your word. You must show me a sign, so I know that the sky lady sends you." And when he heard this, Juan Diego said, "Master, you will have a sign. I will ask her for it."

Then the bishop sent him on his way, and when he had gone, he called in a few of the people who lived in his house and told them to follow the poor man and find out where he went and who he talked to. Well then, so it was done. Juan Diego took to the road, but when he passed through the ravine near Tepeyacac, they lost him and were unable to catch sight of him again. And when they returned to the bishop, they told him that the man was deceiving him, that he had simply dreamed up all the things he had said, and that they would catch him and punish him the next time he came. "Never again will he stand people on their heads," they said.

The next day, Monday, when Juan Diego was to have returned with a sign from the lady, so that he would be believed, he could not go, because when he had come home the night before he had found his uncle, Juan Bernardino, sick to death with the plague. Instead, he went to get a doctor, but it was too late, and that night his uncle begged him to go to Tlatelolco in the morning and bring home a priest to confess him, because he knew he could not be healed.

On Tuesday, very early, Juan Diego left for Tlatelolco to call the priest. When he got to Tepeyacac, he took a different road and passed on the east side of the hill, thinking the lady would not see him. "I will find her later," he thought. "First I must call the priest for my poor uncle." But the lady was there, and she said, "My child, do not be afraid of the plague. Are you not in my lap and in my power? Your uncle will live. I have cured him already."

At this he was greatly comforted, and his mind was satisfied. Then he begged her to send him back to the bishop with proof, a sign, so that he would be believed. "Climb to the top of the hill," she said. "There you will find flowers. Cut them and bring them to me."

When he reached the hilltop, he was amazed to find beautiful Spanish roses blooming out of season, at a time when the frost is harsh. They were fragrant and covered with night dew that seemed like pearls. He began to cut them, then gathered them all, carrying them in a fold of his tilma. When the sky lady saw them, she took them in her arms, then put them back in the tilma. "These flowers will be the sign," she said. "You must take them to the bishop. Tell him to see to it that my church is built."

As he traveled on to Mexico, he was happy, knowing that all would be well. Carefully he held up his tilma in front of him, protecting the flowers and enjoying their fragrance. When he got to the bishop's palace, he was met by the steward and a few other servants. But they would not let him in. Perhaps they recognized him as the one who was always troublesome, or perhaps the others had told them that he had lost them at the ravine. For a long time he stood there, bowed, waiting to be called and as if holding something in his tilma. When they touched him to see what was there, he knew he could not hold them back or else they would push him and hurt him, perhaps kill him. So he showed them the flowers, just a little, and when they saw that they were roses, blooming out of season, they were amazed and tried to seize them and pull them out. Three times they tried, but each time the flowers became no longer real and appeared only as a brocade or a painting on the surface of the tilma.

Then they went and told the bishop what they had seen, and the bishop realized that the sign had arrived that would touch his heart. He gave the order for Juan Diego to enter, and when he came in, he bowed low, just as he had done before. Then he told everything he had seen and heard, how he had asked the sky lady for a sign and how she had given it to him so that he would be believed and the church she desired would be built. "Here it is. Receive it," he said, and he opened the white tilma in which he had folded the flowers. As the roses came scattering out, an image of the virgin appeared on the tilma, just as it is seen today, where it is kept in her blessed church at Tepeyacac, called Guadalupe.

When the bishop and all the others saw the image, they fell to their knees and worshipped it. Gazing at it, they were filled with remorse. It was as though their hearts and thoughts rose upward. Weeping and praying, the bishop begged forgiveness for not carrying out the sky lady's wish. Then he removed the tilma, which had been tied around

Juan Diego's shoulders, and went and placed it in his oratory.

Juan Diego spent all day at the bishop's palace, and the next day the bishop said to him, "Now, you must show me where the sky lady wants her church." He sent out a call for workers to come build it, and Juan Diego showed them the spot. Then he asked permission to go home to his uncle, Juan Bernardino, who had been sick with the plague.

But they would not allow him to go alone and went with him all the way. When they got there, they saw that the uncle was well, not sick at all; and the uncle was amazed to see his nephew accompanied by these people. He asked him why he was being honored in this way, and Juan Diego told him that when he had left to call the priest, he had seen the sky lady at Tepeyacac; she had sent him to Mexico to ask the bishop to build her a house and had told him not to worry about his uncle, because he was cured already.

Then his uncle told him that it was true, that he had seen her just at that time, and she had made him well. Also, she had told him how Juan Diego had gone to ask the bishop to build her a temple. And she had told him to go tell the bishop how he, Juan Bernardino, had been cured and to tell him to give the new church a name. "Let it be called Saint Mary of Guadalupe," she had said.

So Juan Bernardino was brought before the bishop to speak to him and testify. Then he and his nephew, Juan Diego, were given a place to live at the bishop's house until the temple of the royal lady could be built at Tepeyacac. When it was finished, the bishop took the blessed image that he had been keeping in his oratory and placed it in the great church where all the people could worship it. The whole city traveled to see it, and they were amazed; they knew it could never have been painted by human hands. They knew it had been created by a miracle.

The Weeping Woman
The Prince and the Seamstress
Anonymous, 1961

This is the story of a beautiful woman who lived about a hundred and fifty years ago. Later she was called the weeping woman, but in the beginning, she was a humble seamstress, living a quiet life here in Mexico City.

Suddenly one day she met a prince and fell passionately in love with him. A year later a boy was born, and after another year and a half there was a second son. But by this time the prince had left, and it was only if he heard the seamstress was sick or needed something that he would come back to see her.

The day soon came, however, when he could no longer return at all, because his family had made him promise to marry a princess. Still he wanted to help the seamstress, so he sent one of his servants to bring her a few gold coins. Furious at this insult, she demanded to know where the prince could be found, but the servant lied to her and said that the prince had gone to war.

The moment the servant had left, the seamstress threw the coins away and, turning to her two small sons, said angrily, "You are the ones who have caused my disgrace." Then, casting her eyes around the room, she noticed a dagger that her lover had left behind. Picking it up, she ran after the servant, following him to where the prince lived. When she got there, she peered through a window and to her amazement saw the one she loved being married to a princess.

All the way home she cursed the prince, and when she got back to her sons, she said to herself,

"I will end this torment." She raised the dagger that she still held in her hand, killed her children, and buried them in a hole inside her house. Then, fearing that she was covered with blood, she ran to the window, where the lamplight shone in from the street. Seeing the blood, she picked up the dagger again and took her own life. This was exactly at midnight.

Just at that moment the lamplighter was passing by. He saw her kill herself and ran to give the news to the prince. Immediately the prince, who still loved the seamstress deeply, came hurrying to her house. As he rushed through the doorway, the woman stood up and cried, "Alas, my children!"

That's the story, and it is said that this woman still walks along the rivers at night, crying, "Oh, my children!" and that God is punishing her each time she cries.

The Weeping Woman
Cortés and Malintzin
Anonymous, about 1950

Cortés had a son by Malintzin, and when he was to leave for Spain, he said he would take the boy with him. At the thought of giving him up, Malintzin became ill, and for a time she lost her mind. Nevertheless, she kept her child.

When the boy was seven years old, Cortés could not wait any longer. He wanted the boy but not Malintzin, because the boy had Spanish blood. To Cortés, Malintzin was only a mistress and an Indian. In despair, Malintzin killed her son with a knife and buried both him and herself. When her spirit left her body, it cried, "Aaayy!" Ever since, her ghost has been wandering, and people everywhere hear her cry of pain. People call her the weeping woman.

The Weeping Woman
Forever Without Rest
Anonymous, about 1950

She was a woman to whom God had given children, but one day, in a moment of insanity, she threw them into the river. In that instant God ordered her punishment, and she heard a voice saying, "Why have you killed your innocent children? They were given to you to keep. Now you must search for them until the end of the world." And to this day her voice can be heard, often at night, starting about eight o'clock, crying, "Alas, my children!" This is the cry that is heard in the woods and that continues forever without rest.

Notes to the Stories

Sources, here identified in short form, are fully listed in the References beginning on p. 147.

Creation Myths

Page 23 / "The Hungry Woman," retold from the French in "Histoyre du Mechique," ch. 7.

"They thought the earth was a goddess," writes the early missionary Gerónimo de Mendieta, "and they pictured her as a froglike beast with bloody mouths in all her joints, and they said that she ate and drank everything." However, when she wailed in the night she was imagined as a woman, often dressed in white and sometimes with a cradle strapped to her back. In the *Florentine Codex*, the wailing woman appears as half woman and half snake, a picture symbol for the word Cihuacoatl, or Snake Woman, one of the goddess's names. (Mendieta, bk. 2, ch. 4; Horcasitas & Butterworth, pp. 206–7; Sahagún, bk. 8, fol. 3.)

Page 25 / "The First Sun," adapted from two Nahuatl versions in Lehmann, secs. 33 and 1400, and from the Spanish version in "Historia de los mexicanos por sus pinturas," chs. 3–4.

The anonymous author of the "Historia de los mexicanos por sus pinturas" explains that the sun, as we now know it, stops at noon and retraces its path through the eastern sky, sending only its brightness to travel westward until sunset. At night it rests just beneath the eastern edge of the earth, ready to start out again the next morning.

Apparently the first sun was too weak to project light into the western sky. Since the first sun was Tezcatlipoca and the jaguar is one of his disguises, the nightly descent of the jaguar constellation (Ursa Major) is said to represent the sun's fall.

Page 27 / "Monkeys, Turkeys, and Fish," adapted from two Nahuatl versions in Lehmann, secs. 32–35 and 1401–3, and from the Spanish version in "Historia de los mexicanos por sus pinturas," chs. 4–5.

Evidently the trees are imaginary, playing on the names of the two gods. The White Road is the Milky Way.

Page 29 / "Up from the Dead Land," freely translated from the Nahuatl in Lehmann, secs. 1417–40.

Blowing (in imitation of breathing) and circling are magic methods for bringing the dead to life, found in Indian myths and rituals as far north as the Great Lakes. But this myth is also a story about the origin of death. By having the quail nibble the bones, the Dead Land Lord ensures that they will return to him eventually. In addition, the myth justifies the custom of bleeding some part of the body, usually the tongue, the calf, or the penis, as an offering to the gods. The delicate expression "spilled blood from his body" (literally, spilled blood from his member) refers to the penis. Less sophisticated variants appear in "Histoyre du Mechique," ch. 7, and Mendieta, bk. 2, ch. 1.

Page 32 / "True Corn," freely translated from the Nahuatl in Lehmann, secs. 1441–52.

Nineteenth-century anthropologists would have called the interplay between Nanahuatl and the rain gods a nature myth, a myth disguising natural phenomena. Since Nanahuatl is another name for the sun, the story seems to be saying that the sun produces plant growth, which dies if rain does not fall. Like the preceding selection, this myth of the origin of food is included in the so-called *Legend of the Suns,* an important compilation of Aztec myth and history first translated in 1903 (but not made available to scholarship until Walter Lehmann's German-Nahuatl edition of 1938).

Page 34 / "The Fifth Sun," retold from the Nahuatl in Sahagún, bk. 7, ch. 2, from the two Nahuatl versions in Lehmann, secs. 36 and 1453–91, and from the Spanish in Mendieta, bk. 2, ch. 2.

Two further variants appear in "Histoyre du Mechique," ch. 8, and "Historia de los mexicanos por sus pinturas," ch. 7. One of the best-known Aztec myths, this story accounts for not only the birth of the present age, the age of the fifth sun, but the origin of human sacrifice, the most characteristic feature of Aztec religion. Any of the gods might require an occasional human "payment," but the sun had to be nourished regularly with blood from human hearts. For this purpose, victims were laid over a convex stone and held down firmly by four priests, while a fifth cut open the rib cage and extracted the beating heart. Since the ideal victims were prisoners of war, the custom of heart sacrifice became a justification for war itself.

Page 37 / "The Origin of Music," retold from the Spanish in Mendieta, bk. 2, chs. 2–3, and from the French in "Histoyre du Mechique," ch. 9.

Just as the ancient Greeks believed that music was inspired by an unseen "muse," or spirit, Aztec singers imagined their source as a sky spirit, perhaps an ancestor, perhaps a god, or even the sun itself. The singer would "strike up" the song; that is, he would make a tentative beginning. But the spirit would have to give the "answer," thereby "filling the singer's throat."

Page 38 / "Quetzalcoatl in Tula," adapted from the Nahuatl in Sahagún, bk. 10, ch. 29; bk. 3, ch. 3; and bk. 11, ch. 8; and from the Spanish in Mendieta, bk. 2, ch. 5.

Almost every source of Aztec historical lore contains at least a brief description of the great days of Tula. Although the stories are legendary, with Quetzalcoatl often portrayed as the first or last king of the Toltecs, there are decidedly mythic overtones in the suggestion that he served as a culture hero, establishing pre-Aztec civilization as if by a wave of his hand.

The Fall of Tula

Page 45 / "The King's Daughter and the Pepper Man," translated from the Nahuatl in Sahagún, bk. 3, chs. 5–6.

A similar story, preserved in the writings of Fernando de Alva Ixtlilxochitl (vol. 1, pp. 274–85), has the young woman seduced by the king himself, who is said to be her relative. Both stories suggest that loose morals were the cause of Tula's destruction. (Sahagún's account implies that Quetzalcoatl was high priest of Tula, while Huemac was its king. In other accounts, both are kings, serving at different times.)

Page 51 / "The Sorcerer's Dance," freely translated from the Nahuatl in Sahagún, bk. 3, ch. 7.

Perhaps the underlying idea is that the Toltecs abandoned themselves to pleasure, forgetting their responsibilities. According to one account, "there were great famines because of these dances, and therefore the realm was destroyed" (*Il manoscritto messicano vaticano 3738*, fol. 7).

Page 52 / "Master Log," freely translated from the Nahuatl in Sahagún, bk. 3, ch. 9.

A variant has it that the stinking corpse represented the sins of the people (*Il manoscritto messicano vaticano 3738*, fol. 8v). In actual practice, when an Aztec confessed his sins, he would pray out loud, "Hear my stench, my corruption!" (Sahagún, bk. 1, ch. 12). Evidently the Aztecs believed the fall of Tula had been brought about by sin, just as modern Europe blames the decline of Rome on idleness, luxury, and sensuality. See the notes to the two preceding stories.

Page 55 / "The Flight of Quetzalcoatl," translated from the Nahuatl in Sahagún, bk. 3, chs. 4 and 12–14.

This most famous of Aztec legends gave Montezuma reason for thinking Cortés might be Quetzalcoatl, returned at last. A well-known variant, preserved in the *Annals of Cuauhtitlan* (Lehmann, secs. 54–157), has the flight preceded by drunkenness, as here, but with an added sin: Quetzalcoatl calls for his sister, and the two become drunk together. Later, when he has reached the shore, his body is cremated and he, or his "heart," enters the sky and becomes the morning star.

The Founding of Mexico

Page 65 / "The Birth of Huitzilopochtli," translated from the Nahuatl in Sahagún, bk. 3, ch. 1.

The action takes place at Snake Mountain, a town near Tula, where the wandering Mexicans lived briefly before coming south. But Snake Mountain was also the name of Huitzilopochtli's pyramid in Mexico City, and references to the skull rack (where the heads of sacrificial victims were displayed) and the sand moat (a narrow bed of sand at the base of the pyramid) suggest that this may have been a ceremonial myth reenacted on or near the pyramid at regular intervals. In fact, a colossal head of Coyolxauhqui was unearthed in 1830 not far from the site; and in 1978 archaeologists digging at the pyramid's base found a stone disc carved to represent the goddess's dismembered body.

To nineteenth-century anthropologists the story was a "nature myth" (see note to "True Corn," above) in which Huitzilopochtli represented the sun, Coyolxauhqui the moon, and the *huitznahua* the stars; thus we have an allegory of sunrise, in which the emerging "sun" slays the "moon" and puts the "stars" to flight. Certainly the Aztecs were fond of double meanings, but there is no evidence that they had this particular fantasy in mind. It is often repeated, however, by modern writers on Aztec lore.

In a variant, Coyolxauhqui is killed for refusing to lead the Mexicans southward from Coatepec, which would have prevented them from fulfilling their destiny (Durán, ch. 3). Another variant has her killed on a ball court (Tezozomoc, *Crónica mexicayotl*, secs. 44–47).

Page 71 / "Copil's Heart," adapted from the Spanish in Tezozomoc, *Crónica mexicana*, chs. 1–2, Durán, ch. 3, and *Códice Ramírez*, pp. 23–26, and from the Nahuatl in Tezozomoc, *Crónica mexicayotl*, secs. 38–57.

According to one of the sources, Copil's heart was thrown from the very rock where Quetzalcoatl had rested on his flight to the east (*Crónica mexicayotl*, sec. 57). As it lands on the future site of Tenochtitlan, it becomes the forerunner of all the hearts that will later be sacrificed at the pyramid temple of Huitzilopochtli.

Page 75 / "The Woman of Discord," adapted from the Spanish in Durán, ch. 4, and *Códice Ramírez,* pp. 27–30, and from the Nahuatl in Tezozomoc, *Crónica mexicayotl,* secs. 50–83.

"Woman of discord," or *"mujer de la discordia,"* is Durán's translation of Yaocihuatl (literally, War Woman), a name for the earth mother. In one of her rites, prisoners were flayed from head to foot and their skins worn as clothing by impersonators. No one knows the meaning of this practice, but some have suggested that it symbolizes the greening of the earth after the dry season. If so, the boy in the story is participating in a vegetation ceremony, intended to promote the growth of crops. The ritual's immediate purpose, however, is to stir up war by offending the king whose daughter is the victim.

Page 80 / "The Eagle on the Prickly Pear," freely translated from the Nahuatl in Tezozomoc, *Crónica mexicayotl,* secs. 85–92.

The flag of modern Mexico, with its eagle perched on a prickly pear cactus, derives from this mystical legend, representing the site of the ancient city as a holy place dedicated to war. There exists no Aztec commentary explaining the story's symbolism, but it may be guessed that the color white stands for the sun, the eagle represents the sun as supreme warrior, and the lesser birds symbolize its victims. "Crags and caverns" is a figure of speech meaning "place of danger": in other words, the battlefield. "Fire and water" denotes war, "blue" is the color of Huitzilopochtli, "parrot" means warrior, and the prickly pear probably stands for the deserts north of Tula where the Mexican tribe originated. Variants of the legend are in Durán, chs. 4–5, and *Códice Ramírez,* pp. 30–32.

In the Days of Montezuma

Page 87 / "The Talking Stone," retold from the Spanish in Tezozomoc, *Crónica mexicana,* ch. 102, and Durán, ch. 66.

The immovable stone is reminiscent of the immovable corpse in the story "Master Log," above. But while the legends about Tula blame its downfall on drunkenness and loose morals, Montezuma is charged with the sin of pride. The spirit whose warning he fails to heed, here called "our lord who created the sky and the earth," is none other than the Christian God. Naturally, this and all other stories predicting the end of Mexico were composed after the Conquest.

Page 93 / "Montezuma's Wound," retold from the Spanish in Durán, and Tezozomoc, *Crónica mexicana,* ch. 103.

In a similar tale, Montezuma's sister, Papantzin, dies and is laid to rest in a cave, where, returning to life, she hears an angel predict the coming of the Spaniards and the conversion of the Indians to Christianity; when she later reports what she has heard to Montezuma, he is so upset that he refuses to see her again. (Torquemada, vol. 1, pp. 236–39 [bk. 2, ch. 91]; Sahagún, bk. 8, ch. 1.)

Page 96 / "Eight Omens," translated from the Nahuatl in Sahagún, bk. 12, ch. 1.

Although the text was dictated in Nahuatl by an Aztec, the god Huitzilopochtli, in missionary style, is called a devil. The first omen begins in 12 House, a date like Monday the 3rd or Friday the 25th. The sixth omen is the earth mother, Cihuacoatl, in her role as weeping woman. According to Torquemada (bk. 5, ch. 31), "Cihuacoatl . . . was the first woman in the world, the mother of the human race. . . . They say she would often appear with a cradle (*cozolli*) on her back, as though carrying a child or a baby between her shoulders; she would be dressed in white; and when people saw her that way, they took it as a bad omen; and at night they heard the weeping and crying, and whoever heard it shared her pain."

Page 99 / "The Return of Quetzalcoatl," adapted from the Spanish in Tezozomoc, *Crónica mexicana,* chs. 106–8, and Durán, ch. 69.

Perhaps written as late as the 1560s, this account contains much that is historically true, yet it confuses the landing of Juan de Grijalva in 1518 with that of Cortés in 1519, compressing the two events into a single story about the arrival of Cortés. A more sober version, told in Nahuatl, can be found in Sahagún, bk. 12, chs. 2–7.

Page 108 / "Is It You?" translated from the Nahuatl in Sahagún, bk. 12, ch. 16.

Although Cortés was not granted the title of Marquis until later, Indian writers often refer to him by this name when recalling the events of 1519. A briefer account of the famous greeting is included in the codex *Cantares mexicanos* (Bierhorst, song 68, canto A). According to Cortés' own report, "Montezuma came out to greet us with about two hundred of his lords, all barefoot . . . moving in two files against the walls of the avenue, which was very broad and beautiful. . . . And while I was talking to Montezuma, I took off a pearl and glass-diamond necklace that I was wearing and put it around his neck . . . and a servant of his came up with two lobster necklaces wrapped in a towel, made of red bones and shells that they value highly, and from each necklace hung eight gold lobsters of much perfection and nearly a span long . . ." (Cortés, pp. 56–57).

Of the several flowers mentioned in Sahagún's text, only two can be identified: the fragrant white *izquixochitl* or "popcorn flowers" of the Bourreria tree and the magnolia-like *yolloxochitl* or "heartflowers" (*Talauma mexicana*).

After Cortés

Page 115 / "How the World Began," translated from the Nahuatl in Bierhorst, song 58, stanzas 8–20.

Like the Catholic *doctrinas* that inspired it, this brief history of the world is basically a condensation of the Bible, emphasizing the sin of Adam and Eve (which brought death) and the coming of Christ (which promised everlasting life). Little is known of the composer, Don Francisco Plácido, who was evidently a full-blooded Aztec, probably a member of the native nobility. According to the codex *Cantares mexicanos*, which preserves two of his songs, he was Indian governor of Xiquipilco, a town thirty miles west of Mexico City.

Page 117 / "Calling the Ghost of Montezuma," translated from the Nahuatl in Bierhorst, song 70, stanzas 7–10.

Songs of this type were performed as dances to the accompaniment of the *huehuetl* and the *teponaztli*. See p. 13 and the illustration on p. 118.

Page 119 / "The Virgin of Guadalupe," translated (and condensed) from the Nahuatl in Lasso, pp. 24–56.

Many seventeenth-century clerics taught themselves Nahuatl in order to preach to the Indians, studying old manuscripts and borrowing classic figures of speech as a means of improving their style. Luis Lasso de la Vega was no exception. Notice such typically Aztec phrases as "shields and arrows had been laid aside" (first paragraph), "Is this a dream? Am I sleepwalking?" (second paragraph), and "bright as a jadestone bracelet" (third paragraph). In fact, one of the purposes of Sahagún's great work had been to preserve these elegant turns of speech, just so that people like Lasso could learn them and help keep Nahuatl from slipping into a decline. But beneath the verbal embroidery, Lasso's story is little more than a reworking of the Spanish legend associated with the original cult of Guadalupe. It is therefore not an Aztec story, properly speaking—though there will always be people who believe it was written or reported by Aztecs and only copied by Lasso.

Page 127 / "The Weeping Woman," as published in English by Horcasitas & Butterworth, pp. 209, 211, and 218, slightly revised.

The fact that "The Weeping Woman" does not appear in modern Nahuatl folktale collections suggests that it has been kept alive by Spanish-language books and movies. Nevertheless, the folk informants who told these three variants—in Spanish, evidently in response to the question "Who was the weeping woman?"—believed the story to be true. The one about the prince and the seamstress probably derives from a poem by Vicente Riva Palacio. Yet the ultimate source, unquestionably, is Aztec tradition dating from the sixteenth century and earlier. (For the plots of modern Nahuatl folktales, see Horcasitas; for a summary of the poem by Riva Palacio, see Janvier, p. 164.)

Nahuatl Pronunciation

The vowels (*a, e, i, o, u*) are pronounced approximately as in Spanish (*ah, eh, ee, oh, oo*), except that the *o* varies between *oh* (as in English *wrote*) and *oo* (as in *root*). *Cu* is English *kw*; *hu* or *uh* is *w*; *qu* is *k*; *x* is *sh*; and *z* is *s* (as in *simple*). Nahuatl *tl*, whether at the beginning or end of a syllable, is pronounced like the *tl* in *atlas* or *bootleg*, not like the *tle* in *bottle*. As a general rule, Nahuatl words are stressed on the second to last syllable. Thus Mexico is pronounced may-SHEE-ko, not MAY-hee-ko (as in Spanish) or MEK-see-ko (as in English). Observe the following, very rough approximations:

Huemac (WAY-mahk)

Huitzilopochtli (weets-eel-o-POOCH-tlee)

Nanahuatl (na-NAH-wahtl)

Quetzalcoatl (ket-sahl-KO-ahtl)

Tenochtitlan (tay-nooch-TEE-tlahn)

Tezcatlipoca (tess-kah-tlee-POO-kah)

Xochimilco (shoo-chee-MEEL-ko)

Guide to Special Terms

Agave / A large plant with a basal whorl of thick, pointed leaves, also called maguey or century plant. The juice yields pulque, a kind of wine.

Black Chambers / *Tlillan calmecatl,* one of several palaces used by the Mexican kings, perhaps so called because it was near the Tlillan (Black Place), the dark, windowless sanctuary of the goddess Cihuacoatl.

Chapultepec / A hill on the west shore of the Lake of Mexico.

Cotinga / A medium-sized bird with brilliant blue plumage (*Cotinga amabilis*).

Fire Drill / The constellation Gemini.

Guadalupe / Town and shrine of the Virgin Mary, (1) in the Guadalupe Mountains of southwest central Spain, and (2) on the northern edge of Mexico City.

Hall of the Birds / *Totocalli,* building where exotic birds were kept and artisans did their work (Sahagún, bk. 8, ch. 14).

Huitznahua / A name for the early Mexicans (Tezozomoc, *Crónica mexicana*, ch. 2).

Huitzlampa / In a southward direction, the south.

Mexico / Refers to (1) ancient Mexico, an island realm in the Lake of Mexico, made up of the twin cities Tenochtitlan and Tlatelolco; (2) Tenochtitlan only; (3) modern Mexico City, built on the site of Tenochtitlan and Tlatelolco, including the lake bed, now drained; or (4) the modern republic of Mexico, of which Mexico City is the capital.

Olla / Spanish word pronounced OY-ya. An earthenware jar or pot.

Popocatepetl / Smoking Mountain, a mildly active volcano with snow-covered slopes, forty-five miles southeast of Mexico City.

Quetzal / A medium-sized bird with long green tail feathers (*Pharomachrus mocinno*).

Tenochtli / Prickly pear cactus.

Tilma / Outer garment worn by men. See illustrations on pp. 29, 71, above.

Tototl / Bird; figuratively, penis.

Trogon / One of several closely related forest birds, prized for their plumage (Nahuatl *tzinitzcan*). The quetzal (see above) belongs to the trogon family; but *tzinitzcan*, translated "trogon" in this book, undoubtedly refers to a different species.

White Woman / Iztaccihuatl, an inactive, snow-covered volcano next to Popocatepetl (see above).

References

Bierhorst, John. *Cantares Mexicanos: Songs of the Aztecs.* Stanford, Calif.: Stanford University Press, forthcoming.

Codex Mendoza: Aztec Manuscript, with commentaries by Kurt Ross. Miller Graphics, 1978(?).

Códice Ramírez. In Hernando Alvarado Tezozomoc, *Crónica mexicana,* ed. Manuel Orozco y Berra. Mexico: Porrúa, 1975. Reprint of the 1878 ed.

Cortés, Hernán. *Cartas de relación de la conquista de México.* Madrid: Espasa-Calpe, 1970.

Durán, Diego. *Historia de las Indias de Nueva España e islas de la tierra firme,* ed. Ángel M. Garibay K. Vol. 2: *Historia.* Mexico: Porrúa, 1967.

"Historia de los mexicanos por sus pinturas." In Joaquín García Icazbalceta, *Nueva colección de documentos para la historia de México,* vol. 3. Mexico: Salvador Chavez Hayhoe, 1941.

"Histoyre du Mechique: manuscrit français inédit du XVIᵉ siècle," ed. Édouard de Jonghe, *Journal de la Société des Américanistes de Paris,* n.s., vol. 2 (1905), pp. 1–41.

Horcasitas, Fernando. "La narrativa oral nahuatl (1920–

1975)," *Estudios de Cultura Náhuatl,* vol. 13 (1978), pp. 177–209.

Horcasitas, Fernando, and Douglas Butterworth. "La llorona," *Tlalocan,* vol. 4 (1963), pp. 204–24.

Il manoscritto messicano vaticano 3738, detto il Codice Rios. Rome: Stabilimento Danesi, 1900.

Ixtlilxochitl, Fernando de Alva. *Obras históricas,* ed. Edmundo O'Gorman. 2 vols. Mexico: Universidad Nacional Autónoma de México, 1975–77.

Janvier, Thomas A. *Legends of the City of Mexico.* New York: Harper, 1910.

Lasso de la Vega. *Huei tlamahuiçoltica,* ed. Primo Feliciano Velázquez. Mexico: Carreño & Hijo, 1926. Facsimile of the 1649 ed.

Lehmann, Walter. *Die Geschichte der Königreiche von Colhuacan und Mexico.* Quellenwerke zur alten Geschichte Amerikas, vol. 1. Stuttgart: Kohlhammer, 1938.

Mendieta, Gerónimo de. *Historia eclesiástica indiana.* Mexico: Porrúa, 1971. Reprint of the 1870 ed.

Molina, Alonso. *Vocabulario en lengua castellana y mexicana y mexicana y castellana.* Mexico: Porrúa, 1970.

Sahagún, Bernardino de. *Códice florentino.* 3 vols. Mexico: Secretaría de Gobernación, 1979. Facsimile of MS. 218–20, Palatine Collection, Laurentian Library, Florence, Italy. Note: For a Nahuatl-English edition, see Arthur J. O. Anderson and Charles E. Dibble, *Florentine Codex,* 12 vols., University of Utah Press, 1950–82.

Tezozomoc, Hernando Alvarado. *Crónica mexicana,* ed. Manuel Orozco y Berra. Mexico: Porrúa, 1975. Reprint of the 1878 ed.

————. *Crónica mexicayotl,* ed. Adrián León. Mexico: Universidad Nacional Autónoma de México, 1949.

Torquemada, Juan de. *Monarquía indiana.* 3 vols. Mexico: Porrúa, 1975. Reprint of the 1723 ed.

148